THE MORROWS OF ENGLEWOOD

THE MORROWS OF ENGLEWOOD

AN EXTRAORDINARY AMERICAN FAMILY

ALLEN E. HYE

HafniaFL Books

To my beloved grandchildren, Luke and Grace,
in hopes that they too may be inspired by the Morrows'
love of God, family, learning, country, and community.

In *The Morrows of Englewood*, Allen E. Hye presents a compelling narrative that delves into the remarkable lives of Dwight W. Morrow and Elizabeth Cutter Morrow. Through Hye's meticulous research and engaging storytelling, readers are immersed in the story of Dwight's political prominence and Elizabeth's multifaceted roles as an educator, orator, and community leader. Hye beautifully captures the essence of the Morrows' enduring legacy and their profound impact on local communities. *The Morrows of Englewood* is a captivating read for anyone interested in exploring the untold stories of American history and the extraordinary individuals who shaped them.

–**Marek Beck,** PhD, Head of School, The Elisabeth Morrow School

Allen Hye set out to research the man for whom his high school was named. How lucky for all of us readers that he found the extraordinary life and times of Dwight Morrow. Morrow's principles, his scholarship, his diplomacy, his natural curiosity, and his partnership with his wife Elizabeth Cutter Morrow produced a life of service and worldwide friendships.

–**Dr. Frances Levine,** Past President, Missouri Historical Society, St. Louis

I take great pride in being Englewood's longest elected mayor and take my cues from history believing always that "Public Service" is a sacred "Public Trust." This is exemplified in this wonderful work depicting one of Englewood's stellar renaissance leaders and families. The Morrows' indelible mark on our great City and Nation will be felt for generations!

–**Michael Wildes,** Esq., Mayor of Englewood

Much has been speculated regarding Anne Morrow Lindbergh's time spent in solitude on Captiva Island, Florida. Now, through the research of Allen Hye and the subsequent publication of *The Morrows of Englewood*, one can learn of the great Morrow and Cutter families and understand the back story of what may have made the future Mrs. Charles Lindbergh the multifaceted individual she was.

–**Queenie Viglione,** Archivist, Captiva Island Historical Society

Allen Hye takes us through Dwight Morrow's four careers as he becomes a valuable partner in local, national, and international affairs. Although I knew a bit about Dwight Morrow, Hye brings him to life and I have a better understanding of what a special person he was. I especially liked Calvin Coolidge's assessment that Morrow's "plentiful talent" was enhanced by "his character, which was priceless." This book is a must read for Englewood residents, especially school children, who need to know what a fine man Dwight Morrow was and the role that he and his wife, Elizabeth Cutter Morrow, played in our history.

–**Irmari Nacht,** former Englewood Historical Society Co-President and Englewood Assistant City Historian

The Morrows of Englewood: An Extraordinary American Family by Professor Allen E. Hye is a highly readable and meticulously documented compendium of Morrow family highlights and history. Though mainly focused on the careers and accomplishments of longtime Englewood residents Dwight W. and Elizabeth C. Morrow, this compact volume is unique in offering sidelights on other distinguished members of the extended Morrow family. A veritable handbook of professional and family details of four generations of Morrows, parents and siblings, children and grandchildren, with numerous period photos of people and places not previously included in other works.

–**Susan M. Kenney,** Author, PhD, Dana Professor Emeritus of Creative Writing, Colby College, Waterville, Maine

CONTENTS

INTRODUCTION

My particular interest in the Morrows goes back to an extended paper we junior-year students were required to write for our history class at Dwight Morrow High School in Englewood, New Jersey. The monthslong project, which required three book reports and two special "source" reports, was by far the most significant project I undertook in high school. I believed that we students, who were proud to be part of a great high school—stately building on a beautiful campus, solid faculty, diverse and high-achieving student body, outstanding athletic teams—should be conversant about the person for whom it was named. The more I learned about Dwight Morrow the person, the clearer it became that his intellect, character, and accomplishments made him a worthy model for us young scholars. Though I have been gone from Englewood for 60+ years, I still recall with gratitude the experience of attending Dwight Morrow High School and learning about the great man whom I have admired ever since.

Why then revisit this topic so very many years later? For one thing, I still believe that DMHS (and Academies at Englewood) students, staff, and alumni, as well as residents of Englewood

1

should be more familiar with the person whose name—though perhaps not story— they all know. If this book serves that purpose, and if the reader is inspired by a life well lived and is intrigued by the history of an amazing family in our hometown, then I shall be most gratified.

Two other things prompted me to take up again the story that has fascinated me since youth. The first was our 50th class reunion in the fall of 2012. While I did not attend, I read with interest my classmates' e-mails recalling the very special circumstance in which we grew up. From our de facto segregated elementary schools, we blended successfully into one junior high (grades 7 & 8) and high school (grades 9-12). While much of the "adult world" of Englewood still held to old prejudices—in both black/white and Jewish/Gentile issues—and the country was convulsing with the passions of the civil rights movement, our school comprised a balanced community in miniature, a "bubble" someone called it, in a fractured society. This balance was highlighted on the annual Student Government Day in our senior year when a Black female student was elected mayor. I don't recall that we found it particularly noteworthy—she was just one of us, a strong and popular student—until New York television came to cover us, marveling at the contrast between a local "gerrymandering" controversy in Englewood politics and the orderly, color-blind workings of our student government. I was honored to serve as a councilman that day. This event was a source of pride for me, as was attending a school named for such an illustrious citizen.

The second thing that stirred my interest in writing about Morrow was meeting two of his granddaughters several years ago. My wife and I met and spoke briefly about her grandfather with Reeve Lindbergh, the youngest child of Charles and Anne Morrow Lindbergh. Reeve, like her mother, is an accomplished author and the family spokesperson. Later, we met Reeve's cousin, Margaret Eiluned Morgan (cited later as MEM), whose mother, Constance, was the youngest child of Dwight and Elizabeth Morrow. Eiluned, who winters not far from where my wife and I reside in Florida, has been extremely helpful to my Morrow research and a great encouragement.

I subsequently made two visits to the former Morrow estate in Englewood, now the Elisabeth Morrow School, named for their eldest daughter, as well as to Deacon Brown's Point, the Morrow summer home on North Haven Island, Maine. Additional insight into the family's history was gained in the Morrow archives at Amherst College, Dwight's alma mater; at Smith College, where Elizabeth studied and later served as acting president; at Marshall University, where Dwight's father was president; and at the North Haven Historical Society.

These meetings and travels led me further into the Lindbergh story and, almost irresistibly, expanded the scope of this book. Although Charles' fame is universal, it may be for most people limited to the great 1927 flight to Paris and the 1932 kidnapping and murder of his son, Charles, Jr. But there is so much more that warrants mention, starting with the extraordinary partnership between Charles and Anne that adds to our understanding of not only Englewood and New Jersey history, but also of many burning issues of their times, which this study can cover only in brief: the pioneering development of aviation; the loss of privacy in sensational press coverage; pre-war isolationism; World War II on the home front and the battlefield; the challenges of managing a marriage and raising a family; promoting a balance between technological innovation and environmental stewardship. These topics are not only alluded to in writings *about* the Lindberghs, but in numerous works *by* the Lindberghs.

I was also privileged to gain access to more Lindbergh history at the historic Columbus, Ohio terminal and hangar of the Transcontinental Air Transport (later TWA), co-founded by Charles Lindbergh, and to see the Lindbergh kidnapping display at the New Jersey State Police archives in Trenton and the jail and courthouse in Flemington, where the "trial of the century" was conducted in 1935. Finally, living near Captiva Island, Florida has allowed me to use the archival material at Captiva's library and Historical Society and see where Anne Lindbergh secluded herself to renew her spirit and be inspired to write her bestselling *Gift from the Sea.*

It has been fascinating to delve into the history of these families, learn more about their relationship to Englewood, and consider their significance for American history and literature. Before his untimely death in 1931 at the age of 58, Dwight Morrow was a national figure, but most people today, especially outside of Englewood, have never heard of him. Those who have, generally think of him as an ambassador and as Charles Lindbergh's father-in-law, but there is so much more to his story.

So many interesting facts—including and beyond the basics that I recalled from my high school report—have turned up during my research. Often, while anticipating sharing this story with others, I think, "Wow, did you realize that....? Neither did I." For instance, were you aware that:

- Dwight Morrow was a classmate of future President Calvin Coolidge (1872-1933) at Amherst College and later appointed by him to be Ambassador to Mexico? And that it was Morrow, not Coolidge, who was voted "Most Likely to Succeed" by his classmates?
- He had *four* distinguished careers—law, finance, diplomacy, and politics—and was at his death a US Senator from New Jersey?
- Morrow received nine honorary degrees and was offered the presidency of at least one leading university?
- He was *twice* on the cover of *TIME* magazine?
- For the renowned journalist Walter Lippmann, "Morrow qualified as the most talented public man of his generation" (WL2 211)?
- His wife, Elizabeth Cutter Morrow, the distinguished first lady of Englewood, was still living and active in Englewood affairs even as we were in elementary school?
- His daughter Anne was America's first licensed female glider pilot, an accomplished navigator, and the author of numerous books, including six volumes of diaries and letters? That well before we were born, she and Lindbergh were married and lived on and off in Englewood?

When in 1932 the new Englewood High School and the surrounding park were named for Dwight Morrow, most people probably knew of his renown, but not many do today. Someone

Dwight Morrow High School Courtesy Englewood Historical Society

has suggested that a full, scholarly biography needs to be written about him; that may well be, but it will not be my book, nor will this be "another Lindbergh book." Charles is an enormous figure who has been covered in numerous other studies, but he is mentioned here mainly in the context of his relationship to the Morrows, to Dwight and Elizabeth at first and then, of course, to Anne. Rather, I wish to reintroduce to our class and community—and to a wider readership outside of Englewood and New Jersey—a man most worthy of our admiration, recall why we are proud to be alumni of Dwight Morrow High School, and fill gaps in our knowledge of the Morrows and Lindberghs that we wouldn't have known as youngsters.

There are three existing biographies of Dwight Morrow. They are, however, all from the 1930s, so clearly there is room for a new study. The first two biographies were published in

1930, the year before Morrow died. The one work is titled **Dwight Whitney Morrow: A Sketch in Admiration**, by Hewitt H. Howland, editor of *The Century Magazine* and a friend of Morrow's. As the subtitle implies, it is rather brief—under 100 pages—and an admiring personal tribute, written in support of Dwight Morrow's 1930 Senate campaign. A distinguishing feature of the book is its Introduction by former President Calvin Coolidge, a classmate of Morrow's at Amherst College. Coolidge stresses Morrow's "character which was priceless," his public service, and his "conscientious desire to do good."

The other early biography is about twice as long. *The Story of Dwight W. Morrow* is by Mary Margaret McBride, an accomplished writer, interviewer, and media personality, once dubbed "The First Lady of Radio." McBride paints a most sympathetic portrait of Morrow, stressing his character, work ethic, love of family, and his search for wisdom and understanding. While written independently and not for political consumption, it is every bit as positive as Howland's work. Her study covers the basics of Morrow's early life, college training, and the major accomplishments of his career. It concludes with his first speech as candidate for the US Senate the year before he died.

The latest and longest biography, **Dwight Morrow**, published in 1935 by Englishman Harold Nicolson, must be considered the "standard" work on Morrow, but it is also the most problematic. Nicolson had met the Morrows only briefly before Mrs. Morrow commissioned him to write the biography, a "brave gamble," as Nicolson's son, Nigel, concedes. Nicolson lived for extended periods at the Morrow estate in Englewood and was given access to the Morrow papers, the family, and many Morrow associates. He produced a thorough, workmanlike book, but one that lacks the warmth of the first two bios. Morrow, said one family member, "was not well served" by Nicolson's book. David K. Vaughan calls it "irritatingly patronizing" (135). For additional insight into the Nicolson biography and numerous other works that make prominent reference to Dwight Morrow, please consult the Appendix.

This is how my approach will differ from earlier works. Coming 90-95 years after the existing Dwight Morrow biographies, my study has the benefit of including many family updates, seeing how his wife and descendants carried on his legacy and made their own mark on the twentieth century. In contrast to the biographies, I will only briefly summarize the main stages and major accomplishments of Morrow's life, but will add numerous personal details that may be lesser known, yet which contribute to our understanding of a truly remarkable man.

Here are some of the distinctives that this study will include:

- A prominent chapter on Mrs. Elizabeth Cutter Morrow, an extraordinary figure in her own right as matriarch, educator, orator, community leader, and writer—not least as a diarist who documented not only her own life as wife, mother, grandmother, but also the turbulent decades in which America rose from sleeping giant to leading postwar power.

- An expanded account of the Morrows' affectionate relationship to Englewood, including thumbnail portraits of other family members, many of whom settled there, and the who's who list of friends and business associates who were neighbors.

- Information on the Morrows' *three* homes (four including Mexico) that reflect different facets of their active lifestyle.
- A special chapter summarizing the highlights of Anne Morrow's extraordinary partnership with the famed aviator Charles Lindbergh. Like her mother, Anne was a faithful correspondent and diarist whose writings document the American story.
- Numerous pictures, many not reproduced elsewhere, that illustrate both the Morrows' fascinating life and the history that they and the Lindberghs shaped so well.

I hope that the fascination I felt in studying these extraordinarily accomplished people will be shared not only by my Englewood neighbors and classmates but also by anyone who enjoys peeking behind the scenes at lives well lived. By seeing them in the context of their relationship to professional colleagues, to Englewood, and to the broader American culture, I trust that we can also get a special glimpse into the issues and, indeed, the heartbeat of the first decades of the twentieth century.[1]

---

1   Note: The source of quotations will be cited in parentheses with author (or book title) initials and pages, for example: (MMM 16) = Mary Margaret McBride, page 16. See the Bibliography for the full references.

PART ONE
EARLY YEARS

CHAPTER 1

A NURTURING FAMILY

1873-1891

Dwight Morrow was born on January 11, 1873 in Huntington, West Virginia, the third of eight children born to James and Clara Morrow. The three youngest died in infancy, but the five eldest lived noteworthy lives. The parents, known to their offspring by the Latin words *Pater* and *Mater*, stressed the importance of godliness and education in the family. Family prayer mornings and evenings, Bible reading, religious instruction at home, and faithful worship in the Presbyterian church were regular features of the Morrows' lives. Likewise, a love of learning and instruction in academic disciplines such as mathematics, were inculcated in the Morrow children. In fact, all five went on to graduate from college or normal school, paying their own way. It was a remarkable accomplishment in the 19th century when one considers how few Americans, especially women, attended college, and how financially strapped the Morrow finances were.

James E. Morrow Family: rear James, Clara, Dwight; seated Jay, Hilda, Agnes, Alice Courtesy Marshall University's Special Collections Department, Huntington, WV

Here is a brief overview of the family:

- **James Elmore Morrow (1837-1904)** was born in Fairview, Virginia (now West Virginia) and educated at Jefferson College, which later merged with Washington College to become Washington and Jefferson College in Washington, Pennsylvania. After passing the Pennsylvania Bar, he practiced law for but a short time, as civil war had broken out. Morrow served as a captain in the Union army, retiring after being injured in battle. While recuperating from his wounds in Wheeling, he met his future wife, Clara Johnson. They did not marry until after the war, in 1867, by which time he had committed to education as a career. Their son Dwight was born in 1873, while

James served as principal (i.e., president) of Marshall College in Huntington, West Virginia, James' tenure at Marshall was short, and he moved several times to other teaching and administrative positions in West Virginia and Pennsylvania, including as the first president of Slippery Rock State Normal School. His alma mater, W&J, awarded him an honorary doctorate in 1889. He died in 1904 in Englewood, New Jersey, while visiting Dwight, who memorialized his father with a significant contribution to Marshall University that funded the James E. Morrow Library in 1931.

- **Clara Johnson Morrow (1840-1922)** was born in Ohio and raised in (now West) Virginia. She was a woman of faith who "used to tell the children that the Bible

Morrow Library, Marshall University Courtesy Marshall University Special Collections Department, Huntington, WV

15

had been her chief text in learning to read, spell and parse" (MMM 16). From her southern mother, Clara inherited "a certain warmhearted gaiety, a sympathetic tolerance" (HN 5). This stood her in good stead in the demanding job of managing a large family on the small income of her teacher husband. "Yes," she said when complimented on her economical talent, "far too many books; far too little income" (HN 6). Her five surviving children are listed below.

- **Agnes Morrow (1869-1953)** was married to Richard Brown Scandrett (1861-1918) in 1890, and the couple had three children. Her husband, a Pittsburgh attorney, employed his younger brother-in-law, Dwight Morrow, after the latter's graduation from college. Later Morrow would employ his beloved nephew, Richard B. Scandrett, Jr. (1891-1969), as a political aide in his campaign for the Senate. The younger Scandrett, for his part, would name one of his sons after Dwight Morrow and pen a stirring memorial to his uncle at the Senator's death in 1931.

- **Jay Johnson Morrow (1870-1937)**, whose name was derived from his maternal grandfather, John Jay Johnson, was a graduate of the United States Military Academy at West Point and rose to the rank of Brigadier General. After serving in the Philippines, the District of Columbia, and France, he was Governor of the Panama Canal Zone from 1921 to 1924. He married Harriet Butler in 1895, and they lived for a time in Englewood.

- **Alice Morrow (1871-1940),** a graduate of Indiana (PA) Normal School, was a teacher and Resident Trustee at the American College for Girls and its affiliated Robert College in Constantinople (now Istanbul), Turkey. She later lived with her widowed sister Agnes in Englewood.

- **Dwight Whitney Morrow (1873-1931),** named for a famous author and grammarian, William Dwight Whitney of Yale University, was very fond of and kind to his siblings. Several of them joined him in Englewood, and they, along with many friends and institutions, were generously remembered in his will.[2]

- **Hilda Morrow (1874-1954) was** a graduate of Slippery Rock Normal School and known to her grandchildren as a "warm, cuddly, and jolly" person. She married the Rev. Dr. Edwin Linton McIlvaine (1873-1962) in 1890, and the couple had four children. After extensive pastoral service in western Pennsylvania, they eventually settled in Tenafly, New Jersey, next door to Englewood. Dr. McIlvaine, a Presbyterian minister, was a graduate of Washington and Jefferson College, author of a theological study called *The Compass* (1918), stated supply pastor, and later Honorary Pastor Emeritus of the Englewood church in which I grew up, the Community Church on Hudson Avenue.

---

2   See the printed court document of the "Last Will and Testament of Dwight W. Morrow" in the Appendix.

CHAPTER 2

AMHERST COLLEGE

1891-1895

In 1887, at the age of 14, Dwight Morrow graduated from high school in Allegheny, Pennsylvania. After working for four years as a clerk and errand boy in the county treasurer's office, he sought to join his brother, Jay, at West Point. Despite finishing first in the qualifying examination, he was denied entrance when the congressman who held the appointment gave it to another candidate, fearing criticism for appointing two members of the same family. Fortunately, Henry Gibbons, a good friend of the Morrow family and Amherst College alumnus and professor, interceded. He encouraged Dwight to apply to Amherst, and though the youngster struggled with the entrance examination, he was, having been strongly endorsed by Gibbons, accepted on probation, with eight specific conditions to fulfill by the end of his freshman year.

Of course, Morrow fulfilled those conditions, and more, graduating magna cum laude and being inducted into the Phi

Beta Kappa academic honor society. He did so while under constant financial stress, with only very little help from his parents. Brother Jay regularly loaned him money, later paid back with interest, and sister Agnes sent him fine hand-me-down clothing from her well-dressed attorney husband, Richard Scandrett. In addition, Dwight inherited the wardrobe of a graduating fraternity brother. Taking a room at the Gibbons home, and later at that of Professor Anson Morse, helped, and he earned money himself by tutoring other students and winning numerous cash prizes in academic competitions. Some of those prizes for oration, a talent Morrow developed at college. He was a featured speaker at prayer meetings and class banquets, and at graduation he was selected as class orator.

A favorite activity for Amherst students was traveling the 7+ miles to Smith College in nearby Northampton, Massachusetts. It was there in his sophomore year that Dwight Morrow met Elizabeth Reeve Cutter, a bright young lady from Cleveland, Ohio, and his future wife. "When they discovered that the father of each was a Presbyterian elder, they felt it a positive miracle of coincidence" (MMM 37). Still, though they saw much of each other at college proms and other functions, it would be a full ten years before they would marry.

Morrow's time at Amherst, with its superior academic training, and his enduring connection to the college was arguably the seminal experience of his life. Building on the rigor and intellectual curiosity of the Morrow family upbringing, three professors above all shaped his thought and sharpened his acumen. Anson Morse, Professor of History, inspired in him a "quest for historic knowledge" and taught him "to look down the corridors of time" (HHH 10) to find it. History became and remained one of Morrow's great passions, and he shared with Morse the fervent belief in the importance of historical study. After Morrow had graduated, Morse often looked up his protégé when on business in New York. And when Morse's book *Parties and Party Leaders* was published in 1923, it was his former student Dwight Morrow who wrote the Introduction.

His lifelong love of mathematics was fostered by Professor George Olds, who later became president of Amherst. Morrow called him the finest professor at Amherst, while Olds stated that the student "had the best mathematical mind of any man who ever attended Amherst" (MMM 43). Morrow's third great teacher was Professor of Philosophy Charles Garman, whose curriculum took the students from psychology through metaphysics to ethics. He taught his students to challenge any dogma or prejudice they may have and to base their ethical, intellectual, and spiritual convictions on astute questioning and sound reasoning.

In addition to his favorite mentors, Dwight Morrow bonded with some rather prominent classmates. Harlan F. Stone (1872-1946) became chief justice of the Supreme Court, and Bertrand H. Snell (1870-1958) reached the US House of Representatives. Charles D. Norton (1871-1923) became Assistant Secretary of the Treasury and a leading New York banker. He was a great friend and neighbor of Morrow, both in New York and at North Haven, Maine. Most of all it was Charles Burnett (1873-1946) who, for the rest of his life, was his closest male friend and confidant. Burnett earned a Ph.D. at Harvard and became Professor of Psychology at Bowdoin College in Maine. When in 1901 he invited Morrow to meet him on vacation in Annisquam, Massachusetts, it turned out that Elizabeth Cutter happened to be at the same lodge and reconnected with Morrow. Two days later they became engaged, and two years after that they married. Fittingly, Burnett served as best man.

The best-known member of the Amherst Class of 1895 was, of course, the future President Calvin Coolidge, for whom Dwight Morrow campaigned in 1920. Coolidge did not win the Republican nomination, but he was named Vice President and ascended to the presidency when Warren Harding died suddenly in 1923. Coolidge was slow to call on Morrow to serve in his administration, but when he did, in 1925 and 1927, it was with great effect, as we shall see in subsequent chapters.

In the wake of the many prizes and accolades received by Dwight Morrow at Amherst— including graduating magna cum laude and winning two cash awards at graduation—there arose a delightful story that the Class of '95 voted him "Most Likely to Succeed," and furthermore that he received every vote but the one he himself cast for Coolidge. At graduation, Coolidge was Grove Orator and Morrow was chosen as Class Orator. The fact that he commanded such respect in so distinguished a body of future leaders is a wonderful tribute to the character and abilities of Dwight Morrow.

As biographer Harold Nicolson reports, "The love which Dwight Morrow conceived for Amherst remained undimmed until the day of his death" (22). His active support of college events was legendary: Alumni Association; Board of Trustees;

Morrow Dormitory, Amherst College Author's Private Photo

fundraising (more than $3 million in ten days of 1921); the Morrow Dormitory; the Anson Morse professorship; the reconstruction of the chapel; and in his will a $200,000 donation to the college. Beyond the significant financial contributions, Morrow demonstrated his love for and gratitude to Amherst through the time and energy he gave to the college throughout his career. Amazingly, writes Nicolson, who documented the enormous volume of material in the Englewood file cabinets, "some twenty percent of this correspondence is devoted to the interests of his old college" (HN 23).

Finally, it was during his time at Amherst that Morrow developed what is often referred to as his "method," something that characterized every task that he took on in his four careers. Biographer McBride begins with this: "Morrow's method was to get all the facts first. A new piece of business meant first a great fact-finding campaign, research work, talk with individuals. Then, with all the facts at hand, Morrow would move" (84). Nicolson, too, stresses the importance of beginning with fundamentals: "It was Dwight Morrow's custom . . . to approach a problem cautiously and to study it in all its bearings before reaching a decision. Another characteristic was the persistence with which he pursued a problem" (156). Sometimes the factfinding campaign involved hiring experts at his own expense to tackle difficult issues and prepare him for any possible objections that might arise in negotiations. Always it was motivated by his great curiosity and lifelong desire to gain wisdom and understanding in everything he did. In the coming chapters we will see how the Morrow method was brilliantly applied in such varied assignments at the New Jersey Prison Board, the Kennecott Copper Corporation, the three-month study of postwar French economic and social conditions, and his pioneering diplomatic work in Mexico.

PART TWO

FOUR CAREERS

CHAPTER 3

LAW

1895-1914

One of the most admirable qualities of Dwight Morrow was his
versatility, his ability to serve with excellence in so many varied
capacities. His intellectual prowess and incredible work ethic
enabled him to tackle any task and master it in short order. Today
we would say he was a quick study, but in admiring his quickness
one should not overlook the breadth and depth of his research,
his critical thinking, his "method."

This part of our portrait will consider Morrow's four careers
and highlight major accomplishments within each. Think of it—
four careers, each pursued to the highest level, while the rest of
us are happy if we can succeed in one. Once again, I trust that the
reader will be inspired by the prodigious feats of the little man
from Englewood, and again, I hope to make his story accessible
in shorter form, leaving longer, more detailed accounts to earlier
biographers, and adding new information not available to them.

After graduating from Amherst in 1895, Dwight Morrow worked as an apprentice in the Pittsburgh law offices of his brother-in-law Richard Scandrett and lived with his sister Agnes and Scandrett in nearby Allegheny. This was not a happy time for Morrow, who had gone from being celebrated at the top of his class to feeling underappreciated and underused in the limited scope of Scandrett's practice. Continuing to study law and history on his own, Morrow spread his wings and in 1896 moved to New York to study at Columbia Law School. Once again, he put himself through school, living frugally and tutoring younger students in mathematics, often many hours per day during exam times.

One of Dwight's best friends was John Kerr (1873-1962), a Columbia Law classmate with whom he had been acquainted back in Allegheny. Kerr became a patent lawyer in New York, and it was he who first introduced Morrow to Englewood in 1903. Another influential Columbia Law classmate was Johnston DeForest (1873-1952), son of lawyer and financier Robert W. DeForest (1848-1931), whose family was one of New York's wealthiest and most prominent. It was the DeForests, with their opulent downtown and Long Island estate homes, who exposed the poor teacher's son to the high society lifestyle he would later enjoy, not that he sought it out for its own sake. Moreover, the elder DeForest offered the fresh law school graduate a substantial position in New Jersey, with salary starting immediately upon graduation in 1899. This was not to be, but it was surely helpful to have this offer in his pocket as he considered another option.

Morrow's Amherst mentor Professor Anson Morse had advised him to locate in New York instead and recommended him to a friend, Amherst classmate and trustee John W. Simpson (1850-1920) of Reed, Simpson, Thacher, & Barnum (later Simpson, Thacher & Bartlett, which it remains today.) According to established tradition in such circles, Dwight was expected to apprentice in an unpaid capacity, grateful to gain meaningful experience. However, he explained, after seven years of supporting himself through college and law school, he now needed to draw a salary and convinced Simpson to start him as clerk at $60 a month.

Morrow soon began to impress his older colleagues, passing the bar exam in his first year with the firm and earning their respect and confidence, especially in two areas. The first was his clear, precise writing in drafting documents for the firm with great economy of style. As reported by Nicolson, "They were both scholarly and vernacular. There was no attempt to resort to the indolent pedantry of established jargon. . . . The modernity of Morrow's drafting affected the legal correspondence of the time" (93).

Another talent that soon became evident was Dwight Morrow's great facility in negotiation, something that would characterize him in every endeavor. Said Thomas D. Thacher (1881-1950), son of Morrow's employer Thomas Thacher (1850-1918) and himself a distinguished jurist, "He had an uncanny knack of quickly finding the common ground upon which the conflicting claims of divergent interests could be resolved," with both sides "inspired by his integrity of mind and sincerity of purpose" (HN 93). Consequently, Morrow never became a trial lawyer; he argued only a scant handful of cases before the bar. Rather, he worked behind the scenes advising clients, preparing

Dwight Whitney Morrow Courtesy Englewood Historical Society

organizational documents for major companies, and bringing together opposing parties to settle differences.

For four years Morrow established himself as the firm's outstanding clerk before being promoted to "managing clerk" (HN 91) in 1903, the year of his marriage to Elizabeth Cutter. Then, in 1905, having been offered a teaching position at Columbia Law School, he was made partner and served the firm with distinction for another nine years. That Simpson did not want to lose Morrow can be seen in the tribute he paid to him when Dwight's father was visiting in New York. "Mr. Choate, Mr. Root, and I," he told James Morrow, "have the reputation of being the best corporation lawyers in the City of New York. Your boy is better than any of us" (HN 94).

Another example of the esteem in which he was held was the comment by Daniel Guggenheim, the mining magnate and philanthropist whose Kennecott Copper Corporation Morrow had advised so brilliantly. Impressed by Dwight's method of mastering a subject by first researching it from the ground up, Guggenheim declared, "Six months after Morrow had started upon his investigation, he knew more about copper than I or any of my brothers" (HN 149).

The seeds for Dwight Morrow's move from law to the world of high finance were sown in June, 1913, when he gave a speech at the Englewood Armory on behalf of Englewood Hospital, one of his favorite charities. In attendance was Henry P. Davison (1867-1922), a J.P. Morgan & Co. partner who had heard Morrow's name as the banking firm was casting about for a new senior partner the year before, shortly after the death of the company's founder,

J.P. Morgan, Sr. (1837-1913). Impressed with Morrow's speech and with the lawyer himself after a chance personal meeting with him—they locked umbrellas in a rainstorm—Davison consulted with his partner Thomas W. Lamont (1870-1948), an Englewood neighbor and friend of Morrow's, and finally with the firm's new head, J. P. (Jack) Morgan, Jr. (1867-1943). All agreed and offered Morrow a position. As President Calvin Coolidge later remarked, Morgan "told him they wanted him not merely because of his talent, for talent was plentiful and easy to buy, but they wanted him for his character which was priceless" (HHH viii).

Honored though he was to receive the prestigious offer, Morrow still required several weeks—including a retreat to the quiet island of Bermuda—and much consultation with family and trusted friends before accepting. Dwight Morrow was very concerned with what the impact that a life in the world of high finance would do to the values of not only himself but his family members. His wife, Betty's, reassurances on that subject as well as other concerns were very important to him. They were the ultimate team marriage, and her buy-in to this change in their life from lawyers to bankers was critical (MEM). Apparently, one small but decisive factor in Morrow's decision was an editorial cartoon depicting Morgan as a vulture preying on the remains of shareholders of the Long Island Railroad, which Morrow thought unjust and misinformed. His "protective passion for the misunderstood" (HN 128) was aroused, and he was ready to take on a new challenge, one that he met with energy and distinction.

CHAPTER 4

FINANCE

1914–1927

Our earlier description of Dwight Morrow as versatile is never more apt than in considering the thirteen years of his second career, high finance. In highlighting his time as a star at J. P. Morgan & Co., here are but a few of the things we will see him do:

- arrange credit to foreign governments and travel through submarine-infested waters to help the Allied effort in World War I;
- engage in hometown service and lead prison reform in New Jersey;
- spearhead reconstruction in war-torn Europe;
- be offered a college presidency;
- campaign for a college friend as President, even as he considers politics for himself;
- and, in something of a precursor to his next career and to a dramatic change in his family, namely, the marriage of daughter Anne to Charles Lindbergh, chair a landmark committee on the future of aviation in America.

These and other developments will be presented chronologically and in capsule form, understanding that some entries are far weightier than others. Here, as earlier, I refer the reader to previous literature for more details and hope that summarizing Morrow's impressive feats— several of which were done simultaneously—will afford an overview of this era and create a sense of his extraordinary talents, high character, and growing prominence in shaping America's emerging leadership role on the world stage.

1914

On April 15, Dwight Morrow joined the prominent banking firm J. P. Morgan & Co. On July 1, after final settlement of the late Morgan Sr.'s, estate, he was made partner. Five weeks later, the Great War broke out, World War I, which plunged Morgan into a most prominent role in international affairs. First, though, he helped maintain the credit of New York City, which had financial obligations due England and France.

Morrow had no niche at Morgan, as one can see when considering the array of roles that he assumed. Partner Russell Leffingwell explained, "You ask me what was Dwight's function in our office. He had none. He was not charged with any particular duties. He participated in nearly everything we did. His job was to think" (HN 147).

1915–1916

Having already worked with Great Britain and France in the New York negotiations, Dwight Morrow met with financial commissions from those lands to negotiate for them an enormous wartime loan for $500,000,000.

In 1916 he was named Life Trustee of Amherst College, a position he filled with such devotion that Jack Morgan was heard to say that he would give Morrow a hundred thousand dollars if he agreed to "get off that Amherst Board of Trustees" (HH 67).

1917

In January, responding to public and media outcry about conditions in New Jersey prisons, Governor Walter E. Edge appointed Dwight Morrow to a New Jersey Prison Inquiry Commission of five persons investigating the penal system and making recommendations for reform. Morrow immediately began an intensive study of the history of the system and its counterparts in other states, even, at his own expense, hiring two experts to assist him and publishing a bound volume of their findings. When the original chairman resigned, Morrow was chosen to replace him and led the Commission to a final report in January, 1918. This prompted the New Jersey legislature to create a State Board of Control of Institutions and Agencies (1919–1977), which was charged with implementing the far-reaching administrative and, especially, humanitarian reforms that Morrow sought. "His analysis of the defects of the New Jersey system, and the machinery which he provided for an evolutionary improvement, independent of political influences, was, however, so scholarly, so conclusive, so detached, that it served as the pattern for penal reform in many States other than New Jersey" (HN 199). Indeed, in 1920 the National Committee on Prisons and Prison Labor gratefully presented him with a gold medal.

Since 1915, Dwight Morrow and his Morgan colleagues had wrestled with the stubborn problem of how to transform the enormous Equitable Life Assurance Society from a private corporation with millions of policyholders into a mutual corporation owned essentially by those policyholders. The answer came in 1917 in one of what Nicolson calls Morrow's "moods of abstraction" (154) as he walked to lunch with colleague Thomas Cochran (1871-1936) at the Plaza Hotel. So focused on the problem, he veered into Cochran forcing him first toward the street and then against the Fifth Avenue shop windows. Once at lunch, Cochran silently ate his meal while Morrow continued in deep thought, ignoring the dishes that had been brought and taken away. Finally, he hit the table with his hand and announced, "That's done it! I've mutualized the Equitable. Now, Tom, let's go out somewhere and get something to eat!"

Dwight Morrow not only conceived of the intricate process that resulted in the mutualization of the Equitable, he also convinced the other stakeholders to agree to it. This feat "was generally recognized as being one of the most brilliant successes in financial and legal adjustment ever achieved" (HN 155). It was also an excellent example of his enormous powers of concentration, which sometimes were dismissed as only absentmindedness.[3]

To help finance America's involvement in the Great War—the US had entered the conflict in April—the Treasury Department established a National War Savings Committee and in November called on Dwight Morrow to chair the effort in New Jersey. He preached individual thrift, self-denial, and less consumption to

---

3 Delightful stories of Morrow's absentmindedness are legion and included in the Appendix. An occasional one may be apocryphal, but enough of them have affectionately been told by his friends and associates to confirm this trait. Actually, "mood of abstraction," brought about by his extraordinary powers of concentration and focus, might be a more appropriate term.

get urgently needed resources quickly to the front. Only twenty cents a day savings per person nationwide, for 300 days, would, he calculated, make a $6,000,000,000-a-year difference in the amount of capital available for investment (HN 201). Here, as with the prison reform success, his model inspired first New Jersey and then other states, many of which invited him to speak to their citizens.

Morrow framed his message of thrift as call to all citizens to rescue a battered world at war: "The hero of that enterprise will be the plain, old-fashioned man who spends less than he produces, and thus creates the fund without which all of the plans for the restoration of Europe must come to naught. He may be rich, or he may be poor . . . but he must be a saver" (JM 356).

1918

Washington also took note of Morrow's work and in February summoned him to address another urgent wartime issue, namely the lack of coordination among the Allies— primarily the United Kingdom, France, Russia, and the United States—in shipping their men, munitions, and food to the war zone. Allied in name but not always in practice, each nation waged what amounted to its own separate war against the Central Powers— Germany, Austria-Hungary, Bulgaria, and the Ottoman Empire. Their insistence on maintaining sovereignty in their traditional shipping routes and trading patterns was highly inefficient and often dangerous, as some goods unnecessarily wound up passing through a submarine zone when a shorter, safer route was available. President Woodrow Wilson named Morrow advisor to the Allied Maritime Transport Council, which required him to tie up his affairs at Morgan and, along with his wife, take a transatlantic ship through dangerous seas to Europe for meetings in London, where they experienced air raids. They also met in Paris, from where he made numerous visits to General John Pershing's headquarters at Chaumont, about 170 miles from Paris and much closer to the front.

Dwight Morrow began by calculating the tonnage of supplies and the available rail and sea transport, and matching those limited resources to the pressing needs at various points in the war effort. His other great work was to convince the allied nations to pool their resources and work with what he called "intelligent cooperation" to create order out of the shipping chaos while still preserving some autonomy for the allied parties. Morrow's tactful approach convinced especially the skeptical British War Office that General Pershing's requirements for the American Expeditionary Forces (AEF) were not exaggerated but reasonable, and they agreed to the diversion of a half million tons to the American effort. Pershing was so grateful for Morrow's services that he offered him a military commission, and when in the following year Morrow was awarded the nation's Distinguished Service Medal—he was also decorated by Italy, France, and Greece—it was Pershing who presented it to him, with these words: "He was responsible for the first intelligent epitomization of the allied tonnage situation and his able presentation of the situation to the allied countries materially affected the tonnage policy, resulting in all possible economy. By his tact and good judgment in matters affecting the Maritime Board of Allied Supply he helped materially in the splendid results obtained by that organization" (HN 218).

Dwight Morrow had returned home in December and did not go back to France for the Paris Peace Conference at Versailles. He did, however, render great service along with his Morgan colleagues in the reconstruction of Europe in the years after the war.

1919

In January, a scant month after returning from his extended European stay, Dwight Morrow was back at J. P. Morgan. At the same time, he began writing a series of articles analyzing the post-World War I social and political order in light of his profound experiences in the European theater. In February and March, his work appeared in ten installments in the *New York Post*, then was published in a book he titled *The Society of Free States*. The aim of the book, he wrote in the Foreword dated March 20, 1919, "was to review some of the efforts heretofore made to avert war, to consider some of the forces that have been working to bring the world closer together, to give a short account of the growth of the spirit of nationality, and to indicate the conflict between the national aspirations of the separate States and the idea of a League of Nations."

Morrow begins his study with the basic question, "For what has the world fought?" He answers that "even an unprepared world has been able to arise in its wrath to stop—though at fearful cost—the pretensions of autocratic power to impose its will by force upon its neighbors" (6), but that was not enough. Leaders had promised a new world order, "a real European partnership," and an effort to prevent a repetition of the catastrophe. US President Wilson called the conflict the "culminating and final war for human liberty," while British Prime Minister David

Lloyd George maintained, "this must be the last war. . . . an end to all wars" (7). There were calls for a league of nations, a system to prevent future war.

True to his custom of thoroughly researching any topic with which he dealt, Dwight Morrow first summarized previous plans for perpetual peace, beginning with a French proposal from 1623 that stressed the importance of international commerce in preserving the peace and the 1648 treaties that concluded the Thirty Years' War, which tried to establish rules of conduct between nations. He cited other European and American plans that were put forth by such noted figures as William Penn, Jeremy Bentham, Edward Everett Hale, and Jean Jacques Rousseau. The well-attended 1899 and 1907 conferences at the Hague attempted a judicial approach to peacemaking that called for an international prize court comprised of 15 judges, but US participation in such plans often foundered on concerns about American sovereignty. Despite the failure of often utopian plans and numerous treaties over 300 years, Morrow pointed out that from 1914 to 1918 "almost the entire civilized world has combined to resist with arms the treatybreaker. . . . The result of the great war, then, instead of making us despair of international law, should give us added reason for believing in it" (74–75).

But how, on the eve of the Paris Peace Conference about to convene at Versailles, should the victors, facing "a series of problems that will sorely tax human wisdom" (132), proceed as they seek to preserve the hard-won peace? For Dwight Morrow there was no simple solution. A utopian dream of prohibiting war with no international strictures neglects, he reasoned, the drive of human nature to accrue power. The idea of a World-State both disregards the peoples' sense of nationality and raises the question of who is to govern the governors. Rather, statesmanship, communication, avoidance of misunderstanding, and a sense of cooperation are necessary to thread the needle between order and liberty. "The real problem of the Peace Conference," writes Morrow, "is the problem of reconciling the desire of men for world order with their desire to develop their own governments in accordance with their national aspirations" (138). Likewise, "The reconciliation of those two ideals—the ideal of liberty and the ideal of order—is the problem of the statesmen at the Peace Conference. With the whole world as a stage, statesmen are seeking some formula that will bring about ordered liberty" (153–154).

The final pages of Morrow's book reproduce and examine the Text of the Draft of Covenant submitted to the Peace Conference on February 14, 1919 by the League of Nations Committee. He concludes hopefully that if "we build with wisdom, and with courage, and with patience, those that come after us will be helped by our work. Our building may fall, but if we have built aright some of the foundation stones will remain and become a part of the structure that will ultimately abide" (197).

1920

Dwight Morrow's analysis of postwar needs was not merely academic. He warned against American isolationism, and from 1920 to 1927, he and his Morgan colleagues financed reconstruction loans to help a battered Europe back on its feet.

In this year, Morrow received the first of his nine honorary doctorates, and when a Coolidge for President committee was formed, he was an enthusiastic supporter along with other Amherst alumni, though remaining in the background to prevent his Morgan connection from influencing the campaign. However, when the Republican convention met in Chicago in June, Morrow was at the heart of an energetic movement lobbying delegates on behalf of classmate Calvin Coolidge. His endorsement of his college classmate is noteworthy in that it reflects his own values: "For the last year I have been abroad dealing with all sort of government officials. Some of them have been Socialists like Thomas, the great socialist leader in France. Some of them have been from old conservative families. . . . I have about come to the conclusion that the division of the people in the world is not really between conservative and radical, but people that are real people and people that are not. Calvin is one of the fellows who is real. He really wants to make things better not to pretend to make them better" (AS 179).[4] As mentioned earlier, Silent Cal lost the presidential nomination to Ohio Senator Warren Harding, but he was unexpectedly named Vice President and went on to become President when Harding died suddenly in 1923.

On September 16, a wagon laden with iron sash weights exploded in front of 23 Wall Street, the home office of J. P. Morgan and Company. It killed 38 people, including two Morgan employees, and injured hundreds more. Dwight Morrow not only escaped with no injury, but, according to his colleague

---

4   Morrow's reference to the division of people reminds us of his oft-quoted advice to his son: "The world is divided into people who do things and people who get the credit. Try if you can to belong to the first class. There's far less competition."

George Whitney, attributing this to Morrow's legendary absentmindedness, stepped outside to meet a government official, and marched through the wreckage and dead bodies to their appointed lunch. Absentminded or not, Morrow also focused on ushering his guest safely through the traumatic scene, and as one descendant has pointed out, he and his colleagues would almost certainly have established funds for the families of the two Morgan employees killed in the blast.

In late November, amid an economic downturn, Dwight Morrow worked behind the scenes to avert a financial crisis by brokering a reorganization of General Motors, whose chairman, William C. Durant (1861-1947), had vastly overextended himself financially and requested assistance from Morgan in fending off his creditors. From Thursday, November 18 through Sunday the 21st, Morrow, who earlier had voiced alarm about Durant's fiscal irresponsibility, led an intense investigation into Durant's vast and varied holdings and obligations. Working through the night with partners George Whitney and Tom Cochran and with Pierre S. du Pont, a major GM investor, they rescued Durant from a $1,000,000 margin call on Friday, then crafted a plan over the weekend to defuse the crisis by market opening on Monday morning. Durant surrendered over $20,000,000 and his position as GM's head. Du Pont and Morgan funds financed the new, restructured company, which was led initially by du Pont then taken to great heights by Alfred P. Sloan (1875-1966). Sloan's landmark memoir, *My Years With General Motors*, includes a long letter from du Pont that describes the entire affair. It says this about the role of Dwight Morrow and his firm: "They threw themselves into the situation wholeheartedly, stating at the start that they asked no compensation. They have acted with remarkable speed and success, the whole deal involving $60,000,000, or more, having been planned and practically completed in less than four days, in which are included a Saturday and Sunday" (APS 38).[5] Morrow's family remembered it as a wild weekend, with Betty Morrow especially frustrated being in the dark because Dwight could not tell her what was going on.

1921

In January of 1921, Dwight Morrow was approached with a tentative offer to become president of Yale University. Although the academic life was something he had long coveted, he turned it down, as he did with later inquiries from Amherst and the University of Chicago (RC 290). For some time, he had second thoughts about his decision, but soon he was once again involved in international finance.

In February he traveled to France for a three-month study of the postwar situation there. True to his lifelong method of thorough research, he examined the reconstruction first-hand, interviewed leading government figures, employed a subject-matter expert, and reported on major areas of the French economy. His "Memorandum on the Economic and Financial Condition of France" helped skeptical American investors see the need to support the rebuilding of a major wartime ally.

Dwight Morrow's loyalty to Amherst College never waned, and in 1921 it went well beyond cheerleading. He headed a ten-

---

5   See also Ron Chernow's account of the Durant ouster that avoided a market crash (RC 222-225).

day fundraising drive that raised more than three million dollars for his alma mater.

His other international accomplishment this year was helping Cuba establish some order out of economic chaos and collapse. The United States had granted Cuba independence after the Spanish-American War in 1898, but still had legal rights in what was considered a guardian-ward relationship. Morrow's understanding of this arrangement was typical of his sense of fair play and desire to mediate: "This makes it highly imperative that the United States, if they assume the rights of guardian, should also assume the duties; and that means that whenever they administer the ward's estate they should administer it in the interests of the ward rather than in the interests of the guardian" (HN 262). This approach ruffled feathers in high places but helped avert a greater crisis.

Shuttling between New York and Havana, Morrow employed his usual tact and patience in balancing the interests of Morgan, which had issued Cuban bonds that were in danger of defaulting, and the US sugar industry that felt threatened by Cuban sugar production. Lurking in the background, should the Cuban government and economy collapse, was a potential military intervention by the US. This was averted as Morrow first established a cordial relationship with the Cuban strongman President Zayas and then brokered two sizable loans—for $5,000,000 and $50,000,000—that created stability and preserved Cuban independence. As he wrote the following year to the American pro-consul in Havana, "Of course the Government of Cuba has been, and is, very bad. It is possible that the United States might run Cuba much better. As I get older, however, I become more and more convinced that good government is not a substitute for self-government. The kind of mistakes that America would make in running Cuba would be different from those that the Cubans themselves make, but they would probably cause a new kind of trouble and a new kind of suffering" (HN 264–265).

Dwight Morrow's experience in Latin American politics and economics in Cuba would serve him well in a few years when he would assume the position of Ambassador to Mexico.

1922–1924

In 1922, after many years of service, Dwight Morrow resigned from the New Jersey Prison Board. Then in March he, along with his mother, wife, daughter Constance, and sister-in-law Annie Cutter, visited Panama, where his brother, Jay, was Governor of the Canal Zone. Later that year, their mother, Mrs. Clara Johnson Morrow, died at the age of 82.

An important financial project begun in 1922 and completed the following year was a reconstruction loan for Austria, administered through the League of Nations. Morrow's colleagues in that endeavor, with whom he had also worked on the Allied Maritime Transport Council, were Jean Monnet (1888–1979), a French economist and diplomat who for decades effectively promoted European unity, and Sir Arthur Salter (1881–1975), a British economist, politician, and proponent of European unity. Salter's note of May 31, 1923 gives yet another example of the esteem in which Morrow was held by his European colleagues: "Now that, under the lead of Morgan's, an American syndicate has undertaken an issue of the Austrian loan, I want to write to you to

Jay J. Morrow Courtesy Marshall University Special Collections Department, Huntington, WV

Morrow Family 1922 Canal Zone Visit, Rear L to R: Jay, Hattie, Alice, Betty,
Dwight; Front L to R: Dita Butler, Clara, Annie Cutter, Constance Courtesy
Marshall University Special Collections Department, Huntington, WV

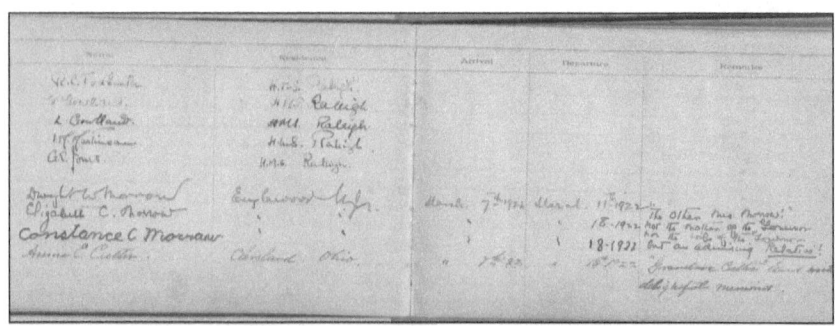

Guest book entry from the Morrows' visit along with Betty's mother, Annie
Cutter, to Canal Zone Governor Jay Morrow. Note Betty's delightful comment
about "The other Mrs. Morrow!" Courtesy Marshall University Special Collections
Department, Huntington, WV

say how much we all appreciate the part you have yourself taken in this great decision. This is much the biggest work the League has yet undertaken; it is much the biggest piece of international construction work undertaken anywhere. And it is very pleasant to think that you and Monnet and I should have renewed our association of the war to take part in this most interesting of post-war jobs" (HN, 244).

In 1923 Dwight Morrow also worked with Amherst colleagues to publish a book by one of his Amherst mentors, the late Professor Anson Morse, a collection of historical essays called *Parties and Party Leaders*. Morrow's scrupulously researched 37-page introduction, was itself a scholarly overview of the origins of parties and put the chapters to follow in the context of Morse's life and exemplary career.

When in August, 1923 Morrow's Amherst classmate Calvin Coolidge ascended to the presidency, it was generally assumed that Dwight would soon be appointed to a high position in his friend's administration; that was not to be, much to the displeasure of Mrs. Morrow. However, one prominent appointment that almost came to be but did not is still of interest to us.

When Germany defaulted on reparations payments after World War I, France seized control of the Ruhr industrial region, forcing a crisis that triggered a new reparations program, the so-called Dawes Plan designed by General Charles Dawes, a banker and future vice-president under Coolidge. The plan called for appointing an Agent General for Reparation, an economic czar to be based in Berlin and manage German payments while guarding against inflation. The European press had called for Dwight Morrow to assume that important and powerful position, and so had Wall Street. "On June 30, 1924, Morrow was informed by the Governor of the Bank of England that his name had been unanimously chosen by the Reparation Commission, subject to the approval of the United States Government" (HN 274). However, when a few days later word reached Morrow from the American ambassador to Germany, Alanson B. Houghton (1863–1941), that some governments would not approve of any J. P. Morgan member, he withdrew his name from consideration. Though initially disappointed, he was probably fortunate not to be involved in the Dawes Commission, about which he had serious reservations: "It is almost inevitable," he said, "that this loan will be unpopular in Germany after a few years" (HN 277).

Sir Arthur Salter, cited above, greatly regretted that Morrow was not appointed and a few years later offered a stirring tribute to the abilities of Dwight Morrow that were, he felt, squandered by the responsible governments: "We needed someone who combined a knowledge of the higher international finance, of the world credit and money system, and of such problems as Reparations and Allied Debts, with sagacity and soundness of judgment, a position of trust and influence in America, and at the same time a profound understanding of the European position and the specific features of the English and French situation and outlook. . . . Morrow combined all these qualities in a degree that I believe to be unsurpassed, and perhaps unequalled, by any living man" (HN 275).

1925–1927

Dwight Morrow's last two-and-a-half years with Morgan would bring him four more honorary degrees, from Princeton, Pennsylvania, Williams, and Yale, but the signature event of this time occurred in a new field, one outside his normal areas of expertise, namely aviation. At the same time, we see the long reach of the White House drawing him toward his third career, diplomacy.

In March, 1925, newly re-elected President Calvin Coolidge had hinted vaguely to Morrow that he "may like to have you look into the subject of airplanes for me" (HN 281), but nothing came of that until autumn in the wake of the crash of the dirigible *Shenandoah* with the loss of 14 airmen on the morning of September 3. This tragedy, plus the inflammatory charges of "incompetence and criminal negligence" in the Navy and War Departments leveled by Col. William Mitchell, head of the Army Air Service, prompted Coolidge to appoint a board "for the purpose of making a study of the best means of developing and applying aircraft in national defense" (MMM 117). On Sunday, September 13, 1925, the nine members of that board—appointed without their previous consent—were announced in the newspapers. The next day, Morrow received a letter from Coolidge, dated Saturday, September 12, summoning him to the White House for a Thursday, September 17 meeting with the President.

When the Board met for the first time that day, Dwight Morrow was elected as chairman and skillfully directed eight weeks of hearings, both in public sessions and in the privacy of his hotel suite. The President's Aircraft Board, the "Morrow

Board" as it came to be known, heard from many constituencies concerned with military aviation: Army, Navy, young aviators, engineers, civilian contractors. All 99 witnesses were granted reasonable time to state their case, including the gentlemanly Orville Wright and the flamboyant Billy Mitchell, the latter taking hours to warn of possible attack by air and urging great investment in an air defense system rather than additional battleships. In an eerie foreshadowing of World War II, Mitchell, in his 1925 book, *Winged Defense: The Development and Possibilities of Modern Air Power— Economic and Military*, had predicted an early morning Japanese aerial attack on Hawaii, striking planes and hangars at Schofield Barracks and then US naval forces at Pearl Harbor. Morrow's role on the Board was featured in the article "ARMY & NAVY: The Air Investigation" in the October 12, 1925 edition of *TIME* with the first of his two appearances on the magazine's cover.

It took some time for the Morrow Board to reach unanimity, but it did, submitting its report to President Coolidge on November 30. They rejected the idea of a crash program for air defense, such as Mitchell would have wanted—after all, were Mexico and Canada any possible air threats? Instead, they tried to reconcile the clash of young and old, past and present that was evident among the witnesses drawn from the military. The Board's report assigned part of the general staff to aviation and separated military from commercial aviation. Assistant secretaries in the departments of Commerce, War and Navy were to be assigned to aviation. It also boosted the morale of military aviators by changing the name Air Service to Air Corps, creating a flying decoration for peacetime service, and making pay and rank comparable to other branches of the armed forces.

Two noteworthy events followed the conclusion of the Morrow Board.

On December 17, after a seven-week court-martial in which he was not judged on the truth or falsity of his accusations, Col. Billy Mitchell was found guilty of violating the 96th Article of War, bringing "discredit upon the military service." He was suspended for five years but instead resigned on February 1, 1926 and continued his campaign for air defense in the private sector.

On December 27, 1925 Daniel Guggenheim, the mining magnate with whom Dwight Morrow had worked in his law practice, founded the Daniel Guggenheim Fund for the Promotion of Aeronautics to speed the development of civil aviation in the United States. Having established his aviation credentials on Coolidge's military board, Morrow would serve as Director on the Guggenheim Fund board through 1926 and into 1927. Among the notables he worked with there were Harry F. Guggenheim, son of the founder, Col. George W. Goethals, Chief Engineer of the Panama Canal, and Orville Wright, the legendary father of powered flight.

1927

After twelve years at J. P. Morgan, Dwight Morrow was ready for a change. He idealized the academic life, but when the chance had come to be a university president, he turned it down. Because of his college friendship with Calvin Coolidge, President since 1923, people had expected him to be tapped for a high position, perhaps in the Coolidge cabinet. Instead, aside from the Aviation Board appointment, there had been relatively little contact between the two men. Morrow took that in stride, and when it was suggested that he might at least be offered a high-profile embassy position such as London or Paris, Morrow demurred. "'No,' he would say when these capitals were suggested, 'my relations with Coolidge are such that I cannot accept an honor from him. But I can accept a job'" (HN 288).

The anticipated "job" was Mexico, but it evolved slowly. In early June, 1927 two threads of Morrow's life crossed in Washington when he was summoned by President Coolidge for two days of meetings at the Patterson House on Dupont Circle, Coolidge's temporary residence while the White House was under repair. First, Morrow, as former head of the Aviation Board, was introduced to the President's guests, Mrs. Evangeline Lindbergh and her son, Charles, who had just returned from his historic flight to Paris. The two men hit it off from the start, and Morrow worked behind the scenes to help Lindbergh and his St. Louis backers pay for the Paris flight, the expenses of which had exceeded their budget.

The original plan was for Lindbergh with his $2,000 savings and St. Louis businessmen with their own investments against a $15,000 bank guarantee to vie for the Orteig Prize of $25,000 to be awarded for the first flight between New York and Paris. However, in his desire to be first, he did not fulfill the required waiting period to qualify for the prize. Even when the registration requirement was waived, Lindbergh wanted the prize to go only to his St. Louis sponsors.

After the flight, Dwight Morrow deftly stepped in and raised $10,000 from his Morgan partners to cover the backers' additional expenses; persuaded them to allow Lindbergh to keep the entire $25,000 prize; and saw to it that Lindbergh's $2,000 savings were returned to him.

Finally, on Morrow's recommendation, Harry Guggenheim and the Guggenheim Fund gave $50,000 to finance the celebrity pilot's three-month tour of the US to promote the development of aviation. Morrow also became Lindbergh's personal financial advisor, and, of course, ultimately his father-in-law (SB 165; TK 133f.; RC 291f.).

Coolidge's major reason for inviting Morrow was to sound him out on the position of Ambassador to Mexico, a tough, unglamorous assignment that Morrow's friends and colleagues advised him to decline. The offer was not formally made until July 14 in a letter from Coolidge, but with yet another delay. It could not be announced before August when the outgoing ambassador would return from leave. On August 19th, Morrow and the President would confer again, this time at Coolidge's vacation site in Rapid City, South Dakota. Having accepted the post, Morrow conveyed that decision in very touching letters to his friend and partner, Jack Morgan, and to his wife, who was most doubtful about the Mexico position.

Citing the President, who felt that he "should probably prevent a good deal of harm if I went to Mexico now," Morrow added, "The upshot of it was that I told him he was the President and that if he thought I ought to go, I was willing to go." Morrow closed his Morgan association with this personal tribute to the firm's head: "I want you to know, dear Jack, that I am not doing it without a very real sorrow at leaving, and a very great pride in having been associated with you during these years" (HN 291).

Betty Morrow's great concern about the move was assuaged by Dwight's note reiterating the President's desire for him to take the post and his intention to accept it if she would accompany him. Her diary notation for August 26, 1927 illustrated the depth of their partnership and set the tone for their highly successful stay in Mexico: "This afternoon such a beautiful letter from Dwight telling about his talk with the President. There is one golden sentence in it—one word of balm so perfect to my heart! 'This appeals to me more than Yale or the Reparation job or International Law at Columbia.' I would go after that—if I had to crawl to Mexico!"

CHAPTER 5

DIPLOMACY

1927–1930

On September 20, 1927 Dwight Morrow was commissioned by President Coolidge as Ambassador Extraordinary and Plenipotentiary to Mexico. He and his wife put their plans for a new Englewood home on hold and bade farewell to a host of well-wishers as they and daughter Constance left in a private railway car for the great diplomatic challenge ahead. On October 21 they crossed the border at Laredo and arrived in Mexico City on October 23.[6]

The President's basic instructions to the new ambassador were "to keep us out of war with Mexico" (HN 314). Indeed,

---

6 Shortly after crossing the US-Mexico border, the train stopped to allow passengers to get out and stretch their legs. This also permitted the Morrows' beloved West Highland White terrier, Daffin, to be taken off for a walk. When the dog slipped his lead and began trotting back north, one of the travel party remarked rather too loudly that Daffin was the only member of the party that showed any sense. Daffin was caught and the train continued on what daughter Constance recalled as "the longest train trip in the world" (MEM).

there was precedent for such a task in the cordial relationship Morrow had established with Cuban President Zayas in 1921 to avert the potential military intervention that was in the offing. "Is there anyone," he wrote at that time, "who thinks that if a man owes him money and cannot pay it, there is profit in going out and killing him?" (RC 292). In Mexico, whose violent political past and worsening relations with the United States presented a far greater and more complex challenge, all his intelligence, tact, and wisdom would be required.

Here are a just few key dates to illustrate this turbulent history:

- 1836 – Battle of the Alamo, a major event in Texas's drive for independence.
- 1844 – US annexation of Texas, which was admitted to the Union in 1845.
- 1846–1848 – War between the US and Mexico.
- 1910 – Beginning of the Mexican Revolution, with years of armed revolts, political coups, and assassinations. Scholars variously date the end of the Revolution as 1917, 1920, or even 1940.
- 1916–1917 – Military incursion by revolutionary Francisco "Pancho" Villa into New Mexico prompts an unsuccessful US expedition into Mexico, led by General John J. Pershing.
- 1917 – Mexican Constitution is adopted. Article 27, which states "ownership of the lands and waters within the boundaries of the national territory is vested originally in the Nation, which has had, and has the right to transfer title thereof to private persons,

thereby constituting private property," proves highly controversial, both internally and externally.

1927

The ten years preceding Dwight Morrow's arrival in Mexico were filled with tension and threats of war, aggravated by a strict interpretation of Article 27. The *New York Herald Tribune* wrote in December, 1926: "With American rights being trampled underfoot in Mexico, in the view of the administration, but with the American public almost militantly opposed to any backing of the firm stand already taken, President Coolidge and Secretary of State Kellogg are at a loss as to the next move in the situation" (SR 276).

By the time Morrow arrived in Mexico in 1927, he had to contend with the country's lingering issues such as these:

- Newly defined subsoil, or mineral, rights, especially oil, on lands owned by foreigners.
- Mexican zoning laws that prohibited foreign ownership of land near the border or the coasts.
- Government sanctions against the Catholic Church, a strike by clergy that suspended religious services, and armed rebellion by a Catholic militia called Cristeros.
- Confiscation of American-owned land without proper compensation.
- Default on foreign debt.

Even though the American public was in no mood for war, many Mexicans feared that Morrow, a J. P. Morgan partner, would be looking out only for the vested interests of American banks and investors—and would be ready to use force to protect them. "After

Morrow, then the Marines," one newspaper lamented. They need not have worried, for Dwight Morrow wanted to work with the Mexicans as peers, not treat them as wards or rivals. He wished to help them solve problems and lead them to prosperity, not dictate terms or impose "solutions." Instead of the heavy-handed approach too often used by his predecessors, Morrow desired to craft a statesmanship based on respect for the people, their sovereignty, and their culture. Before heading south, he famously said, "Well, *I* know *one* thing I can do for the Mexicans. I can like them" (MMM 128). This he did so genuinely that even those critics wary of his appointment embraced him and his family.

It helped that Morrow, through his time with Morgan, was quite familiar with Mexico's finances, particularly the difficulty in paying off their foreign debt. Beyond that he had thoroughly researched major disputes between the US and Mexico—even to the point of hiring expert advisors at his own expense—but those issues were not his first order of business. Rather, he sought to establish cordial personal relations and gain the trust of his counterparts, beginning with President Plutarco Elías Calles (1877–1945).

Calles had played an important role in the Mexican Revolution as both a politician and a general, helping depose dictator Porfirio Diaz in 1910 and fighting rebels such as Pancho Villa. In 1917 he became governor of the state of Sonora and again participated in a coup that brought General Álvaro Obregón to power in 1920. After four years of cabinet level service, Calles was elected president in 1924. His regime was marked by harsh measures against the Catholic Church and strict laws about outside ownership of Mexican land. Both issues put him at odds with financial and clerical interests in the United States. He could have been a formidable opponent for the new American ambassador, but Morrow did not approach him as an opponent. Nor was Calles looking for a fight. The president knew of Dwight Morrow's reputation as a man of high character and was eager to establish a good relationship with him. He also received a personal letter from the Cuban president praising Morrow for his work with Cuba years before (RM 5–6). Calles thus made every effort to hail the ambassador's arrival as the promising beginning of détente.

The achievement of Morrow's mission was laid early on. In his public statements he acknowledged Mexican sovereignty and told his countrymen, "It is essential that we understand our neighbors. The secret of success in international relations is being able to see the good in the other fellow" (SR 281). Quoting former Secretary of State Elihu Root, he also urged American businessmen in Mexico to respect their hosts: "You not only represent your country, but you have a duty to perform toward the country in which you live. . . . While you continue to be good, loyal American citizens, you should be good and loyal Mexican residents" (SR 279). Recognizing that the Americas are made up of countries besides the United States, Morrow changed the name of his residence from "American Embassy" to "US Embassy" and his own title to "US Ambassador to Mexico" (RM 9).

Within a week of his arrival, Morrow began building bridges with President Calles. They met on October 29 and again on November 2 for breakfast at the president's farm. No staff was present but the president's interpreter, allowing for a more personal exchange. Another get together followed on November 6, at which time the men discussed Calles's irrigation plans, a key factor in the development of northern Mexico. This kind of personal, almost folksy approach was soon labeled by an admiring press corps as "ham-and-eggs" and "shirt-sleeve" diplomacy. Calles then invited Morrow to join him on a seven-day, 3,000-mile inspection tour of the north,[7] including visits to agricultural schools and dams.

The wildly popular American entertainer and columnist Will Rogers (1879-1935) also joined the tour, and the cowboy philosopher's good humor further promoted collegial feelings between the president and ambassador. "I did not invite Will Rogers to Mexico," Morrow said, "but when he got here I did grab him and he was of a great deal of use" (Ross 279). In an apt parallel to Morrow and his desire to "like" the Mexicans, Rogers' well-known motto was "I never met a man I didn't like," so the two Americans made a fine team. It was on this trip that a legal solution to the oil rights dispute—seen as a phenomenal accomplishment for Morrow—was worked out, and the news of a budding friendship was reported through the press. "A man with heart has come to Mexico as ambassador from the United States" (MMM 135), said one statesman. President Calles added, "I consider Ambassador Morrow a good friend. . . . I am happy that he is the Ambassador to Mexico and that improvement in the relations between the two countries is being effected" (SR 280).

At about the same time, however, a violent church-state confrontation arose when a bomb was thrown at General Álvero

---

7   See newsreel footage of Morrow's visit to a ranch at https://digital.tcl.sc.edu/digital/collection/MVTN/id/2016/rec/5.

Obregón. The general was unhurt, but the four men found guilty of the attack, Father Miguel Pro Juárez and three associates, were executed on November 23. By publicly demonstrating his friendship with Calles—including inviting him to be the first Mexican president inside the US Embassy— Morrow knew he would open himself to criticism by those outraged over the execution and the government's continuing harassment of the church. Indeed, Morrow was harshly criticized in the short run but felt that gaining the trust of Calles was vital to his mission. "Terrible" though he found the execution to be, Morrow still stated, "I am accredited to General Calles and if I am to accomplish anything in Mexico I cannot start by offending him" (cited in RM 8). That strategy proved to be correct.

The visit of celebrity aviator Charles A. Lindbergh in December, 1927 was an even greater triumph for the new ambassador. While working with J. P. Morgan, Dwight Morrow had become Lindbergh's financial advisor. In gratitude the aviator said, "if, by any chance, an opportunity should arise when I might be of any aid to you, please call on me" (ASB 172). Indeed, there was such an opportunity, and Morrow was quick to seize on it. He proposed a goodwill tour to Latin America, with the celebrated *Spirit of St. Louis* taking a safe, leisurely route to Mexico, stopping along the way in the Caribbean. Lindbergh, however, believed that a non-stop flight from Washington, DC to Mexico City would have a much greater impact and insisted, "You get me the invitation, and I'll take care of the flying" (ASB 172). And that he did, navigating by dead reckoning, struggling to follow railway lines and the towns they connected, dipping

DWIGHT W. MORROW
ENGLEWOOD
NEW JERSEY

October 4, 1927

My dear Colonel Lindbergh:

Thank you heartily for your letter of September 29th. The appointment to Mexico came in such a way that it seemed clear to Mrs. Morrow and me that we should accept. What we can accomplish there, I do not know. Apparently the situation is quite confused. You spoke to me once about the possibility of your doing a little flying in Latin-America. Possibly when you get back from your trip and have a little rest it would be worth while for us to take it up. It would be a fine adventure.

I congratulate you upon the way your trip has gone. I was out West for a few days this summer, and I was struck by the amount of publicity that was given by the local papers to your trip. I think I told you when I first met you in Washington that the United States was farthest behind in airports. I think you have made a wonderful contribution in that field, and we are all indebted to you.

With reference to the investment of your funds, I know that J. P. Morgan & Co. would be very pleased indeed to help you. I have told Harry Davison to put himself entirely at your disposal in this respect. Accordingly, if and when you have some money to invest you send it to J. P. Morgan & Co. and write on the outside of the letter "Attention of Mr. Henry P. Davison", it will receive immediate attention.

With kindest regards to your Mother when you next write her, believe me,

Faithfully yours,

Dwight W. Morrow

Colonel Charles A. Lindbergh,
    c/o The Daniel Guggenheim Fund
    For the Promotion of Aeronautics, Inc.,
    New York City.

Letter from Dwight Morrow to Charles Lindbergh congratulating the aviator on his historic flight and inviting him to Mexico Courtesy Missouri Historical Society Collections

Lindbergh Prepares to Land in Mexico on December 14, 1927 Courtesy Missouri Historical Society Collections

Charles Lindbergh with Ambassador and Mrs. Morrow and their daughter Constance Courtesy Missouri Historical Society Collections

down to read the town names on railway stations and comparing them with a simple map. The worried ambassador, his family, and President Calles had been waiting at the airport for nearly six hours. They, along with a joyous crowd of 150,000, were much relieved when, Lindbergh safely landed on the afternoon of December 14, after more than 27 hours of flying.[8]

Lindbergh stayed at the embassy for two weeks, accompanying the Morrows and their four children in social and sightseeing activities. The aviator's mother, Evangeline Lodge Land Lindbergh, was flown from Detroit to Mexico City to join the party, and Charles used that plane to take members of the Morrow family and President Calles up for their first flight. Lindbergh's presence made a big impression on the Mexicans and, it turned out, on the ambassador's middle daughter, Anne: a thoughtful, scholarly student from Smith College who was spending Christmas break with her family.

On December 28 Lindbergh left Mexico for an ambitious and highly successful tour that covered 16 countries in South and Central America and the Caribbean, where the aviator continued to be showered with praise and gifts by adoring fans. For him, it was an excellent opportunity to showcase the possibilities of aviation and encourage its development. For the ambassador, it was a goodwill tour, a fitting conclusion to his extraordinarily successful first few months of diplomatic service.

---

8   See newsreel footage of Lindbergh's arrival at https://digital.tcl.sc.edu/digital/collection/MVTN/id/7997/rec/3.

Dwight Morrow with a potter in Oaxaca, Mexico Courtesy Amherst College
Archives and Special Collections

1928–1929

Another gesture of goodwill that marked the Morrows'
relationship to the Mexicans was their genuine affection for the
culture. In their second year, they purchased from Frederick
W. Davis (1880–1961), an American ex-patriot and local
businessman specializing in silver crafts, a small home in the
town of Cuernavaca, about 50 miles south of Mexico City.[9] They
went on to acquire adjacent properties and add additional rooms
created by a native craftsman under their supervision. They
named their beautiful home Casa Mañana, a play on their family
name and the Spanish word for 'tomorrow.' (The Morrows later

---

9   See newsreel footage of their home at https://digital.tcl.sc.edu/digital/collection/
     MVTN/id/2340/rec/4.

employed the same pun at their new Englewood home, calling it Next Day Hill.)

The Morrows spent weekends in Cuernavaca, a welcome getaway from the big city, but the retreat also proved to be an excellent place to receive guests and do government business in the more relaxed fashion that Morrow preferred. The Morrows took great pleasure in furnishing and decorating the home with high quality Mexican pieces such as chairs, tables, wooden bowls, sarapes, and pottery. Casa Mañana was also graced by patios, fountains, and terraces with lush fruit trees. The Morrows' collection now resides at the Mead Art Museum at Amherst College. It is chronicled in a richly illustrated book edited by Susan Danly, *Casa Mañana: The Morrow Collection of Mexican Popular Arts*.

Also helping in outfitting the home and connecting the Morrows to the local culture was, in addition to Davis, another American ex-pat, William Spratling (1900–1967), an architect, artist, and renowned silversmith. At Dwight Morrow's suggestion and with his backing, he successfully revived the silver industry in Taxco, Mexico, where his silverwork and archeological collection is housed in the William Spratling Museum. Mrs. Morrow later worked with Bill Spratling on an illustrated 1932 book about her house, *Casa Mañana*, and for years she continued the financial support initiated by her husband (MEM).

There was also René d'Harnoncourt (1901–1968), an Austrian count, commercial artist, and curator living in Cuernavaca who in 1930 created the pictures for Mrs. Morrow's children's book, *The Painted Pig*. With Morrow's help and encouragement, he also put together in the US a celebrated exhibit of Mexican art. After a hugely successful 1930 debut in New York, d'Harnoncourt took the exhibit to seven more cities in 1931 and another six in 1932. Morrow's support helped launch d'Harnoncourt on a successful career that culminated with his becoming director of New York's Museum of Modern Art.

Through these friends Morrow also established relationships to prominent Mexican folk artists, especially Diego Rivera (1886–1957) and his young wife, Frida Kahlo (1907–1954). In a show of support for Mexican culture, Morrow commissioned Rivera to create an extensive mural for the Palacio de Cortés in Cuernavaca, the 16th century palace built for Hernán Cortés, the Spanish explorer who conquered the Aztecs and claimed Mexico for Spain. The mural depicts in several frescoes the history of the state of Morelos from the Spanish conquest up to the Revolution of 1910. But before agreeing to create the mural in the Palacio de Cortés, Rivera demanded and received full artistic control over its content. Morrow's one demand was that Rivera depict one of the priests as a good one. The artist complied with a very small image of a blind priest tucked away in a lower corner of the fresco (MEM). One might have expected tension between the communist Rivera and the former banker Morrow, but the opposite was true. While Rivera was painting the frescoes, the Morrows allowed him and his wife to live at Casa Mañana, which the artists greatly enjoyed. In fact, according to one family member, they were so comfortable there that they almost revised their communist beliefs.

After Dwight's death in 1931, Betty Morrow kept her Mexican home and retained Fred Davis to manage it for her. She returned to Casa Mañana almost every year for a month's visit, and later donated funds to restore the Rivera murals (SD 87).

There were two significant developments in the Morrow tenure in Mexico that were present in 1927 but persisted through 1928 and well into 1929: 1. the ongoing problem of agrarian reform and 2. another flare-up of the intense church-state relations. Both initiatives were stalled by a political crisis, but Ambassador Morrow was successful in eventually negotiating a settlement.

1. Agrarian Reform

President Calles's grandiose plans for agrarian reform involved appropriating property from large landholders, for reasonable compensation, and redistributing it among small farmers, *campesinos*, who, he hoped, would thrive in communities supported by government investment in schools, banks, roads, and irrigation. Calles called this his "integrated solution" to the agrarian problem in an "era of reconstruction" that would consolidate the gains of the Revolution (SR 11). The challenge for him was twofold: if he moved too slowly, the militant *campesinos* might accuse him of betraying the Revolution. If he moved too fast with land confiscation, then there would be less money available to compensate landowners, develop the desired infrastructure, and address the country's serious debt problems.

Dwight Morrow also walked something of a tightrope, wanting on the one hand to respect the Mexican laws that permitted land reform and on the other to advocate for the many US landowners, that they might receive adequate compensation for their lost property. He also wanted to counsel moderation with Calles and advise him on the dangers of accelerating land confiscation. To do this with more effect, Morrow enlisted various Mexican government officials to accompany him and his staff on fact-finding missions to investigate first-hand particularly thorny disputes and come to a mutually agreeable settlement. They travelled an astounding 10,000 miles, visiting every Mexican state. The results were satisfying verdicts for many US citizens and reasonable compromises for some others. Land distribution was drastically reduced in 1928, and more reductions were budgeted for 1929 (RM 12–13).

Progress in agrarian policies, however, was halted with the assassination by a religious fanatic of General Álvaro Obregón on July 17, 1928. Obregón had been the designated successor in the presidential election scheduled for the end of Calles's term, November 30, 1928. This put Calles in a bind as he tried to solve the question of succession while facing both aggressive agrarians wanting more and faster land redistribution and the reactivation of Cristeros violence. An interim president was named, Emilio Portes Gil (1890–1978), a former governor and strong proponent of agrarian reform, and the election was postponed until November, 1929.

Richard Melzer explains how Dwight Morrow greatly aided Calles in four main ways:

1. By making a speech to the US Chamber of Commerce in Mexico City expressing his "absolute confidence in Mexico's ability to resolve its 'great problem' by the 'orderly process of law'" (14).

2. By making "a tour of Puebla and Oaxaca to prove that the Mexican countryside remained peaceful. . . Morrow's successful trip not only alleviated US fears, but also helped to deter internal troubles" (14–15).

3. By attending and enthusiastically endorsing Calles's speech on September 1,1928, which declared that "the time had come to create a government based on laws and institutions—rather than on strong personalities" (15).

4. By strongly supporting the Mexican government in the succession crisis when a military revolt, the so-called Escobar Rebellion, broke out on March 3, 1929, led by General José Gonzalo Escobar (1882–1969). The rebels lobbied in vain for US support; to the contrary, Washington sent substantial military aid to the government forces of Interim President Portes Gil and General Calles, who remained as *Jefe Máximo* (supreme leader). Morrow supported their efforts "making the US Embassy look more like general's headquarters than an ambassador's chambers" (15–16).

On November 17, 1929 Calles's candidate, Pascual Ortiz Rubio (1877–1963), was elected president. This resolved the succession crisis and pleased both Morrow and the US government, not least because it led to another significant reduction in land redistribution. Dwight Morrow's tactful support of Calles, Portes Gil, and Ortiz Rubio, while advocating for US landholders in the agrarian problem, was also evident in the ongoing struggle between the Mexican government and the Catholic Church. These complex issues ran parallel to each other, and in both cases the ambassador was able to negotiate compromises that benefited both sides.

2. Church-State Relations

For centuries since the Spanish Conquest in the 1500s, Mexican church-state relations had been more than strained, and they came to a boil in 1926 when provisions to the 1917 Constitution were enforced requiring Catholic clergy to register with the state—in effect making them civil servants, and, they feared, threatening to institutionalize atheism. With encouragement from the Vatican, clergy refused to comply with the order and went on strike, suspending religious services. At the same time, the disaffected churchgoers called Cristeros formed an armed militia to battle government troops, and their campaign came to be known as *La Cristiada*, the Cristero Rebellion. As noted earlier, there was a violent episode right after Dwight Morrow's arrival in Mexico, but beginning in January, 1928 he endeavored to mediate an understanding between American Catholics, represented by Father John J. Burke, who were distressed at the plight of their Mexican brethren, and President Calles. Later, at Morrow's urging, Mexican bishops represented by Monsignor Leopoldo Ruíz were also allowed to participate. Secret negotiations began in April but were interrupted first in May by an embarrassing leak to the press by Ruíz, and then on July 17 by the assassination of General Obregón. Morrow made repeated attempts at reconciliation—not only with Calles and provisional president Portes Gil, but also with the Vatican. This initiative was so important to Morrow that he stated, it would, if successful, be "the greatest thing I have ever done" (ECM 4/3/28).

With the outbreak in March, 1929 of the Escobar Rebellion and renewed Cristeros activity, the time was ripe for another initiative, and this time it succeeded when President Portes Gil on May 2 and Archbishop Ruíz on May 3 publicly announced their willingness to compromise. When in June Ambassador Morrow returned from his daughter Anne's wedding in Englewood to Charles Lindbergh, a draft agreement was reached and shortly thereafter approved by the Vatican. The Church agreed to call off the strike, register priests, and resume religious services, while the government promised it would permit priests to give religious instruction and would not try to destroy the Church and impose atheism. As Harold Nicolson explains, "Morrow never claimed that this agreement was more than a temporary armistice. . . . He did not solve the Catholic question in Mexico. All he did was to ease the deadlock, to lay down a basis for future cooperation and negotiation, to enable the Church without loss of face to resume religious services, and to rid the Government of the dangers of the Cristeros and the Defense League, while diminishing the odium with which they were regarded in the United States and Europe" (HN 346).

Nonetheless, Morrow's role after almost *eighteen months* of negotiation is most impressive—his "greatest diplomatic triumph" according to historian Arnold Toynbee (HN 339)— especially when one considers how he, a non-Mexican and non-Catholic, so successfully brokered an understanding between two hostile Mexican forces while also alleviating the serious concerns of American Catholics and the Vatican. The Mexican people certainly recognized that, showering honors upon the ambassador in communities all over the land. A humorous footnote was reported by Morrow friend and legal advisor George Rublee (1868-1957). On Sunday, June 30, 1929, awakened from sleep by fireworks and Cuernavaca church bells tolling to celebrate the resumption of services, the ambassador quipped to his wife, "Betty, I have opened the churches. Now perhaps you will wish me to close them again" (RC 296).

1930

Despite two additional triumphs—in international and New Jersey politics—1930 was not a good year for Dwight Morrow. In November, 1929 two assignments were offered to Morrow, one to serve on the US Delegation to a Naval Disarmament Conference in London, the other to run for the position of US Senator from New Jersey. Though still ambassador, he accepted both. While he distinguished himself in both capacities, the two triumphs damaged his relationship to Mexico, and the cumulative stress wore him down physically and emotionally. In addition, a dispute with his Morgan colleague Thomas Lamont, which had begun in 1928, boiled over in late 1929 and continued into the summer of 1930.

3. The Lamont Feud

Mexico's debt had been in default since 1914, and much of it was held by J. P. Morgan, whose clients were demanding repayment. Upon assuming the post as ambassador in 1927, the fair-minded Morrow had determined not to be viewed as a debt collector for the world of high finance. To that end, he distanced himself from his Morgan partners, especially in the question of foreign debt. His approach to the problem was to consider all three groups of Mexico's creditors, which included Morgan's bondholders, western US railroads, and Mexican lenders. Morrow worked with the US State Department to pursue a comprehensive plan along the lines of a general bankruptcy settlement where all claimants would receive some satisfaction. Lamont, on the other hand, wanted his investors to have first crack at whatever funds were available and he sought to cut a private deal directly with Mexico (RC 297). As it turned out, writes Ron Chernow, "Mexico kept postponing the date of debt repayment, and the whole farce would collapse by 1932. The outcome would have been laughable had it not consumed so much of Lamont's life and impoverished small Mexican bondholders" (RC 299).

4. The London Naval Conference

Especially after the horrors of the Great War, world disarmament plans seemed more necessary than ever. The London Naval Conference of 1930 was the third of five meetings between the world's leading naval powers seeking to establish limits on their warships while respecting the members' security concerns and their desire to save on military expenditures. The five nations meeting in London were the United States, Great Britain, France, Italy, and Japan. President Herbert Hoover appointed Dwight Morrow to the prominent American delegation, which consisted of politicians, diplomats, naval officers, and advisers.[10] They departed for London on January 9, and the conference convened on January 21. It closed with a signed draft on April 22.

---

10   See newsreel footage at https://digital.tcl.sc.edu/digital/collection/MVTN/ id/5556/rec/1 and https://digital.tcl.sc.edu/digital/collection/MVTN/id/ 7196/rec/2.

Initially, it was France that, desperately concerned for its security, was consistently threatening to leave the meeting until Dwight Morrow, well informed about French circumstances and a master at conciliation, convinced them to stay. Later, other disputes arose between the various parties, and in March the conference appeared to be deadlocked, but Morrow's tenacity again proved decisive in bridging the divides that existed between the delegations. One biographer colorfully described his unique contribution as a "combination of driving power and lubricant," adding, "It was Morrow who, when the Treaty had to be cast in final shape, was appointed chairman of the drafting committee" (HN 374). Furthermore, under his urging, the Treaty took only four days to complete, rather than the ten that had been projected because of the Easter holidays.

Here is a concise summary of the conference results:

"The London Naval Treaty did not achieve all that had at one time been expected. Yet it did exclude, and forever, the danger of Anglo-American naval rivalry. It did achieve a temporary solution of the Japanese problem. It contained many useful stipulations regarding the humanization of submarine warfare. It did much to clarify confused thinking on such subjects as global tonnage and categories. And it did create a naval holiday [moratorium] in respect of capital [largest] ships. It saved Great Britain an expenditure of some £60,000,000, it saved the United States some $500,000,000, and Japan some £13,500,000" (HN 375).

This tribute from Morrow's colleague Sir Arthur Salter, echoing the sentiments of others, attests to his accomplishments in bringing about these results: "Had it not been for Morrow, there would never have been an agreement. He was the most important of all the Delegates" (HN 357).

5. Candidate for the Senate

When in January, 1929 the idea was floated that Dwight Morrow might be appointed Secretary of State by President Hoover, he discouraged such talk, stating that his place was still in Mexico. His initial reaction was the same when a New Jersey member of the Republican National Committee and Englewood neighbor, Daniel E. Pomeroy (1868–1965), called him on November 26, 1929 to ask him to serve as US Senator, first to fill the unexpired term of Walter E. Edge (1873– 1956), who was appointed Ambassador to France, then to run for the six-year term that followed. Morrow's advisers had mixed feelings. Betty liked the idea but had concerns that proved prescient: "I am really only afraid that after the chance is gone Dwight will regret it. It would be a fine dignified life—and we would leave here before Dwight's prestige wanes" (ECM 11/27/29). Along with Governor Morgan F. Larson (1882–1961), Morrow worked out what he thought was a tentative plan to have David Baird, Jr. (1881–1955) fill the unexpired term and then, if all were in agreement after the Naval Conference concluded, run for the new term and finish Morrow's work as ambassador. However, word of the arrangement came out in the newspapers, causing Morrow much distress. "Last night was terrible!" Betty wrote. "Dwight hardly slept at all. He talked and talked about the senatorship. He feels very unhappy over it. He thinks he has been tricked into apparently making a decision. He feels that he should not hurry away from Mexico and that above all he should not have his hand forced into making a decision of such importance in a hurry and at a long distance" (ECM 12/3/29).

Morrow's discomfort continued after he returned from the London Naval Conference on April 29, 1930, successful but worn out. Having agreed, under some compulsion, to run for the US Senate, he immediately had to engage in the primary campaign, which was already well underway, having been launched while he was in London. The burning issue on which he had to take a stand was Prohibition, and though some advisers counseled maintaining the status quo, Morrow took a clear, principled stand in favor of repeal of the 18th Amendment. Once again, Betty documented the anguish he felt at the way the candidacy had evolved: "Dwight is so tired; so discouraged; so *wild* that he has been trapped into this Senatorial campaign. He is exhausted, does not want it, would be glad to lose. . . . Dwight is sick with regret that he has ever gone into this thing" (ECM 5/13-14/30).

Dwight Morrow's opening speech in the campaign, "Prohibition, a Problem in Government," was delivered in Newark the following day, May 15, 1930 to great applause. Reasoning that Prohibition works best in states where it corresponds to the people's sentiment and works worst in areas where the people and officials do not support it, he advocated full repeal and a policy of letting individual states decide for themselves whether to allow or prohibit the manufacture and sale of alcohol.

"I believe," he said, "that the way out of the present difficulty is to recognize clearly the fundamental difference between the nature of the Federal Government and the

State Government. I believe this involves a repeal of the 18th Amendment and the substitution therefor of an Amendment which will restore to the States the power to determine their policy toward liquor traffic. . . . I look forward to the time when the moral teachers of the country will realize that in this world-old battle for a great social reform there was wisdom in the system of experimenting in forty-eight laboratories rather than in one" (MMM 180, 183).

The campaign was another triumph for Morrow: he won the June 7 primary election by more than 300,000 votes. But when he returned alone to Mexico on July 3 (his wife had stayed behind in Englewood to support Anne and her new baby, Charles A. Lindbergh, Jr.), he found that Betty's concern about his prestige waning had already proved true. He was coolly received, and though he did depart on cordial terms, he no longer had the same warm relationship to his Mexican colleagues.

We can point to four reasons why:

1. Morrow's prolonged absences for the Havana Conference (January–February, 1928) and especially for the London Naval Treaty (January–April, 1930) were perceived as neglect of his diplomatic duties in Mexico City.

2. His absence during the Senatorial primary campaign was seen as further evidence of neglect, and his willingness to run for the Senate was alleged to be a sign that he had merely used the diplomatic post as a stepping stone for his political ambitions.

3. The current Mexican president, Ortiz Rubio, had not been part of Morrow's "magic" in the first two years

and thus was not so inclined to give him the benefit of the doubt when criticisms arose about his supposed influence over Mexican finance that appeared to disrespect Mexican sovereignty. Many Mexicans were tired of hearing stories of Morrow's legendary accomplishments, as if their own president had not also contributed to them significantly.

4. Most damaging of all were the intemperate comments by Colonel Alexander "Sandy" Macnab, former Military Attaché at the US Embassy, in a campaign speech on April 23, 1930, while Morrow was still out of the country. Trying to impress his Newark audience with the ambassador's great accomplishments, Macnab unwittingly implied that Mexican leaders were quite incapable of managing their own affairs. Morrow had, he said, "put Mexico on her feet and given her a strong Government." Furthermore, "There is no department of government in Mexico which he has not advised and directed. He took the Secretary of Finance under his wing and taught him finance" (HN 382).

In the final ten weeks of his term, despite efforts to reconnect with colleagues and to publicly praise and encourage Mexico, Morrow's effectiveness had waned. Dwight Morrow departed Mexico City on September 17 and, after a westward tour, returned to Washington, DC on September 30, when he formally resigned his post.

6. Legacy

Despite the final disappointments, Dwight Morrow's diplomatic legacy remains strong. One need only recall that he created what amounted to an armistice at a time when there were rumblings of war; a quick resolution of the oil crisis; the public relations coup of Lindbergh's goodwill visit; brokering a peace between church and state; and creating a warm bond to the Mexican people and their culture. Morrow himself conceded that he could effect no permanent solution to all of the US-Mexico disputes, nor could he compel Mexico to heed each of his suggestions to lead them to prosperity. Still, virtually all historians acknowledge that his tenure as ambassador was seminal in improving relations between the two countries and setting the tone for a more enlightened US foreign policy in Latin America. One historian described his respectful and compassionate approach to diplomacy as a "precursor of Franklin Delano Roosevelt's Good Neighbor Policy of 1933–45," while another called him "the genius of the new diplomacy" (RM 20).

Dwight Morrow was the right man at the right time, for both Mexico and the United States. Morrow, wrote Mexican studies scholar Stanley R. Ross, "initiated the correct approach for his country. Sympathy, understanding, confidence, and cooperation constituted the only practical policy, the only alternative to legal controversy, threats, and the employment of force" (SR 289).

TIME magazine must have agreed, for at the conclusion of Morrow's term, it put him on the cover of their September 29, 1930 issue.

CHAPTER 6

POLITICS

1930–1931

This final chapter on Dwight Morrow's four careers is necessarily short, covering the Senator's less than one year in office. After resigning his ambassadorship, Morrow returned to Englewood for much needed rest, then began his second electoral campaign of the year on October 8. He handily won the November 4 general election by 200,000 votes. On December 3 Dwight was sworn in as senator to replace David Baird, Jr. in filling out the unexpired term of Senator Walter E. Edge through March 3, 1931. Then his full six-year term commenced on March 4.

The first few months were "not an enlivening experience either for Morrow or his wife" (HN 390). She faced social obligations as a Senate wife, including attendance at Ladies of the Senate events; he had to adjust to a totally different routine. The laudatory press that accompanied Dwight's arrival in the Senate must have been an irritant for his new colleagues, just as many Mexican politicians chafed under the stories of his

Morrow Senate Primary poster Courtesy Marshall University Special Collections
Department, Huntington, WV

legend. Whereas he was used to researching thoroughly any problem that he tackled, he was now called on to cast votes on all manner of issues that he had not had time to master in an arena that he viewed as superficial. Believing that "a baby Senator should be seen and not heard" (HN 388) and, he said, "simply serving his apprenticeship" (O&I 291), Morrow humbly took his place on the back bench, declined committee appointments, brought no motions to the floor, and, taking the long view on his new position, immersed himself in an extensive study of parliamentary procedures.

Shortly after beginning his full term, he was again called on to serve as expert troubleshooter. Even as Morrow was on his way to vacation in Italy, Secretary of State Stimson implored him to interrupt his trip in London to mediate in another naval dispute between France and Italy, which he did from March 16 to 18. After returning from his European getaway on May 5, Senator Morrow was a frequent visitor at the White House as financial adviser to President Hoover. The Great Depression had set in, and there were recurring fears of inflation and of economic collapse in Europe that would further damage the American economy.

The summer was spent at the North Haven, Maine home, where Morrow bid what turned out to be his final good-bye to daughter Anne as she and Lindbergh left for their pioneering, months-long flight to the Orient. Even in the idyllic setting of his island home, "it was impossible to make him rest" (HN 397). A vascular spasm on September 10 may well have been another symptom of Morrow's relentless schedule, lack of sleep, and growing worry about the world's financial problems. His final demanding days bear witness to that.

October 1, 1931 saw Morrow once again on his way to Washington to meet with Stimson. The Secretary asked if he would agree to head the US delegation to the World Disarmament Conference planned for Geneva in 1932. As with the initial call to serve in the Senate, Morrow agreed, but with reservations.

On October 2, after dining with Stimson, Morrow took an overnight train to New York.

His traveling companion, a Mr. John Marshall, later recalled: "He seemed to find satisfaction in the thought that his appointment would give reassurance on the other side of the water. He said more than once, 'John, that was a compliment, wasn't it?' I asked him if he would like to go and he said, 'No! I had hoped they would send [Senator William Edgar] Borah.'...In the morning I said to him, 'Mr. Morrow, did you sleep?' He said, 'Not very well; I kept waking up thinking what a hell of a mess the world is in'" (HN 399).

On the afternoon of October 3, Morrow hosted a reception at his home for Senator Baird, shaking hands for hours with over 5,000 (!) people. And in the evening, he was feted by the Bergen County Committee.

His relentless schedule never let up. On Sunday, October 4, he and Betty drove to Englewood's Winton White Stadium to review F Company of the 104th Engineers, New Jersey's National Guard. And that evening in New York he delivered an after-dinner address, carried by local radio, appealing for funds to benefit Jewish charities. Early the following morning, October 5, 1931, Morrow suffered a cerebral hemorrhage at his home and never regained consciousness. Betty was with him when he drew his last breath.

Elizabeth Cutter Morrow Courtesy Englewood Historical Society

Morrow's funeral, planned by Betty and Elisabeth, was held two days later at First Presbyterian Church. It was attended by numerous dignitaries, including former President Coolidge, with throngs of mourners—Morrow's Englewood neighbors and friends—and newsreel cameramen circling the church outside.[11] Mrs. Morrow's diary records several elements of the service:

- Hymn: "For All the Saints Who from Their Labors Rest"
- Two Psalms: 90 and 121, the latter a family favorite that the Morrows regularly recited together, beginning: "I will lift up mine eyes unto the hills, from whence cometh my help. My help cometh from the Lord, which made heaven and earth."
- Socrates prayer from Plato's *Phaedrus*, a Dwight Morrow favorite, which said, "May the outward and inward man be at one."
- A few verses from Philippians 4, including verse 8: "Finally, brethren, whatever is true, whatever is honorable, whatever is just, whatever is pure, whatever is lovely, whatever is gracious, if there is any excellence, if there is anything worthy of praise, think about these things."
- Another hymn: "Dear Lord and Father of Mankind." After the service, the flower-draped coffin was borne from the building to a hearse for transport to Brookside

---

11 See newsreel footage of the event at https://digital.tcl.sc.edu/digital/collection/MVTN/id/7196/rec/2 and https://www.pond5.com/stock-footage/item/75769004-wealthy-businessman-and-ambassador-dwight-morrow-given-final.

Cemetery, mere blocks down the hill from the Morrow estate, for burial at three o'clock. Betty was greatly comforted by the service, the beautiful flowers and gravesite, and the "outpouring of love and devotion! The whole world sending messages of admiration and condolence! I never expect to see anything like it again" (ECM 10/7/31).

Of the many public tributes to Dwight Morrow, two deserve special mention here. The first is by *New York Herald Tribune* journalist Walter Lippmann, a Morrow advocate and sometime adviser in Mexico. Lippmann's October 7, 1931 remembrance in the paper was reprinted later in *Public Persons*, a book of essays on prominent twentieth-century figures.

Lamenting the shallow state of public discourse in the years after World War I, Lippmann wrote,

"The historic achievement of Dwight Morrow was that he broke through these conventions of insincerity in public life and raised a standard of intrinsic worth to which men could repair. Like the greatest teachers, he taught by example. . . . No man of our time has had the complete trust of so many different kinds of people" (WL 106–107). About Morrow's unique blend of trust and intellect, Lippmann wrote, "The peculiar genius of Dwight Morrow lay in the fact that he kept a mystical faith in men without losing his own intellectual standards. . . . He lived at a pitch of mental activity many stages above that of the normal actively-minded man. His brain never stopped going and it never was aimless" (WL 107–108). Lippmann closed by citing Morrow's "ultimate wisdom about human affairs. . . . Thus it was in the art of honest dealing that he was a master, and an example to his country" (WL 109).

The other special tribute was offered by the US Congress in a publication that documented the May 25, 1932 memorial services for three senators and sixteen representatives who had passed away during the last year. The volume dedicated to Dwight Morrow contains the text of the composite service— prayers, music, formal address—that was celebrated in the House of Representatives for the nineteen decedents. It also includes the individual tributes offered in his memory. Some of those recount the many professional accomplishments that this study has examined, while others stress the extraordinarily high esteem in which Morrow was held by his political and diplomatic colleagues. Both New Jersey Senators, Morrow's successor Hamilton F. Kean (1862–1941), and W. Warren Barbour (1888–1943), eulogized their late colleague.

One especially distinctive contribution to the volume was from an October 14, 1931 memorial gathering at the American Embassy in London. Chaired by Ambassador Charles G. Dawes, who offered the first tribute, it included remarks by ambassadors from France, Italy, and Japan, plus representatives from Mexico, the British Foreign Office, and the American Press Association. There were also comments from two distinguished friends, Montagu Norman, Director of the Bank of England, and Charles Selden of the American Press Association. What follows is a selection from the many tributes in the Congressional memorial volume.

"His passing closed a long and brilliant career of useful public service to his own State, to the Nation, and to the people of other nations, and bereft the world of an international figure whose wide sympathies, keen intellect, sound judgments, and wise counsels were never more greatly needed to help civilization find its way out of an economic and social morass" (Kean 39).

"Nature seldom decorates a man of genius with those human qualities and that exceptional character which were possessed by Dwight Morrow and which are really needed to give high ability its greatest effectiveness and usefulness in the world" (Dawes 46).

"The characteristic of Dwight Morrow, as he comes to my mind, was good will. He felt a very earnest good will toward the work he was doing and an extraordinary good will toward anyone who was associated in that work. That good will was helped in the most remarkable way by a sort of movement in his mind—what we call in French 'verve.' He had verve, and he had courage, which is always a great characteristic in these serious times of our lives. He had, too, what was very peculiar, a curious absent-mindedness which added to his personal charm" (Fleuriau 49–50).

"His keen mind, his perseverance, and his remarkable power of easing the tense atmosphere, whenever it was endangered, were most essential in those anxious days. The cause of the peace and prosperity of the whole of humanity will suffer in the loss of this great American statesman" (Matsudaira 51–52).

"Within a very short time of the opening of the [naval] conference, there was, I believe, no man who had a better mastery of those problems. . . . When he crossed the ocean to come to this country, he had already won our great esteem and admiration. When he left, he carried away with him our deep affection as well" (Craigie 55).

"Few men have devoted themselves so unreservedly to the public welfare as did Dwight Morrow. In his hands any problem was assured of a safe and sane solution. His passing leaves the world bereft of a charitable figure, a true gentleman, a talented statesman, and a heart which beat in accord with all of humanity" (Barbour 58).

PART THREE

FAMILY AND HOMES

CHAPTER 7

ELIZABETH CUTTER MORROW

1873–1955

That such an extraordinary man as Dwight Morrow would have an extraordinary wife should be no surprise. She was indeed a remarkable woman and is herself worthy of a complete book, not just a chapter. Of course, there is already a book about her early life, on which we will draw, but her later biography is a fascinating study as well.

Though one can legitimately call the Morrows the "perfect couple" or "team," it took them quite some years to figure that out before they married at age thirty. We can see many similarities in their early lives: their financially stressed upbringing, their love of family, love of learning, their ethical values, and their deep religious faith. In the all too brief 28 years of their life together, we also see a great partnership that built a beautiful, highly accomplished family and helped lead America through turbulent times. It was, wrote one columnist, "my favorite love-success story," which featured Elizabeth Morrow "in her best role, that of loving wife to a man whom she had helped rise from poverty to riches and fame" (MMMO). But after Dwight was gone, she continued to shine as mother, grandmother, educator, church leader, and civic benefactor.

In highlighting her life, this chapter will rely primarily, though not exclusively, on two sources. The first is her daughter Constance's delightful book, *A Distant Moment: The Youth, Education, & Courtship of Elizabeth Cutter Morrow*, which takes her up to age thirty. Betty's extensive diaries are another trove—including the published book covering 1927–1930, *The Mexican Years*. The diaries not only cover her life with Dwight Morrow and illuminate what we have said about his biography, they also share her perspective on the stormy decades that followed.

1. Cleveland and Beyond

Elizabeth Reeve Cutter was born in Cleveland, Ohio on May 29, 1873, to Annie Spencer and Charles Long Cutter, a young attorney. Betty, or Bessie, as she was known to the family, had a twin sister named Mary and three younger sisters: Annie Spencer Cutter, born in 1877 and named for her mother; Rose, born in 1885, and Edith born in 1887. Mary was underdeveloped compared to Betty and in chronically poor health. Diagnosed with tuberculosis of the hip, Mary spent her last years as an invalid and died in 1882. The following year, Betty's parents, out of concern for her health, sent her to live with a great-uncle and prominent Dayton physician, Dr. John Charles Reeve (1826–

1920).[12] While there, separated from her parents and sister, Betty began her lifelong practice of letter writing and keeping a diary.

Two other uncles served as patrons, even as her father fell on hard financial times. Her father's brother, Arthur Cutter, treated Betty to all sorts of gifts, stories, games, and stimulating activities—including a trip to Washington, D.C.—and became one of her favorite correspondents. Uncle Charles Dillingham, Aunt Frances (Fannie) Cutter Dillingham, her father's sister, and their daughter, Pauline, also broadened Betty's horizons by inviting her to their New Orleans home in the winter and taking her on stylish family vacations to places like Texas, Colorado, and Chicago. Betty grew quite fond of the good life and comfortable railway travel, conceding as a young teenager, "Private cars are my weakness" (CMM 24).

Two quotes from these years reveal much about the resolve that would characterize the adult Betty. To her cousin Pauline she wrote in 1887, "If I feel I *must* do a thing, I generally manage to do it" (CMM 27). And the following year, Dr. Reeve assured Mrs. Cutter, "She has improved vastly, and she gives promise of being a bright active and useful woman. I think I can see that she will be fully capable of taking care of herself" (CMM 34). Indeed, she was, as was demonstrated when she prepared to enter college.

Betty Cutter pursued an active academic and social life at Cleveland Central High School and was anxious to attend Smith College, a prominent women's school in Northampton,

---

12   Dr. Reeve, among many other accomplishments, introduced the oral thermometer to the US after his studies in Germany and was a pioneer in the use of chloroform in the US as an anesthetic after his studies in London (MEM).

Massachusetts. However, she realized that her frequent absences from school while living and traveling with the Dillinghams had left some gaps in her education. To remedy that and prepare for Smith's rigorous entrance examinations, she enrolled in Miss Mittelberger's School, a prestigious and demanding private institution in Cleveland that had already sent pupils to Smith. Told that she was unlikely to achieve the needed certificate in one year, she poured herself into her studies, and, to help pay her way, took a tutoring job. She was successful and told that upon passing a German examination once on campus, she would be formally admitted to Smith.

2. New Life at Smith College

Betty Cutter's relationship to Smith was every bit as meaningful to her as was Dwight Morrow's to Amherst. As soon as she bid farewell to her parents, "she walked into a new life which was to affect every event of her subsequent history and color every attitude until her last hour of consciousness" (CMM 61). Two impressive figures immediately gave her the assurance that she was right where she belonged. The dignified Laurenus Clark Seelye (1837–1924) was Smith's first president, now in his eighteenth year. Nicknamed "Prexy" by the students, he imparted a sense of stability and security to the young Betty, especially as he led worship. "When I saw Prexy march down the aisle at my first chapel, I knew everything was all right" (CMM 63).

Armed with a letter of introduction from a prominent Cleveland academic, Betty immediately sought out Professor of English Mary Augusta Jordan (1855–1941). She found a devoted teacher and sharp wit whose concern for and personal engagement with her students was legendary. Colleagues revered her with such words as "the brightest pearl" at Smith, "she's little, but she's fierce," and "the most vivid personality on the campus" (CMM 77, 79). Betty began with an intensive writing course and continued to sharpen her intellect and her writing under Miss Jordan for all four years. Jordan routinely invited students to her home to discuss their work and their personal lives. "For many students, of which Betty was one, this unusual accessibility and avowed interest in the girl's own experience, was the most significant feature in Miss Jordan's teaching" (CMM 80).

Just as Betty had delighted in dances and parties in Cleveland, she gladly joined in the social life at nearby Amherst College. At the end of April, 1893 she made the acquaintance of an Amherst sophomore named Dwight Morrow, and in June they met again with several other couples for a lively outing with dinner, dancing, and a coach ride. Their relationship almost didn't survive that good time, for in May Betty learned that her parents had fallen on hard times and could not afford to send her back to Smith in the fall.

Fortunately, her beloved Uncle Arthur could, and he paid for her sophomore year. This was another parallel to Morrow, whose siblings stepped in when their parents could not foot the bill at Amherst. Betty's relationship to Morrow continued with occasional dates to football games, even as they maintained the formal mode of address, "Mr. Morrow" and "Miss Cutter." But while Dwight was interested only in her, Betty was not as willing to tie herself down. Her reluctance increased when Uncle Arthur died in the spring of 1894, and she withdrew further.

Betty's junior year, her favorite, was marked by three things:

- being named literary editor of the *Monthly* campus journal, for which she wrote a regular column.

- making the acquaintance of another editor, Amey Owen Aldrich (AOA), who became a lifelong friend. Interestingly, Amey's brother, Chester, also became a friend of the family and served as architect for the Morrows' later homes at Englewood and North Haven, and for the fateful Lindbergh home near Hopewell, New Jersey.

- hearing Dwight Morrow proclaim his love for her. He was, said one of her classmates, "tongue-tied with love." This came shortly before his graduation, and dreading the thought of not seeing her again, "he poured out all his feelings and hopes" (CMM 115– 116).

Dwight's feelings were not reciprocated, but he did obtain permission to write to Betty, though only "*occasionally.*" The letters are a key to their future relationship.

The summer of 1895 in Cleveland was not a pleasant one for Betty. Burdened with family chores and already concerned about life after college, she wrote to a classmate, "I can't bear to think of coming home for good, and I hate the life here" (CMM 119). Those concerns remained after return to Smith in the fall. "[H]er senior year was a paradoxical mixture of many flattering college honors and painful anxiety about how effective her abilities would be in the frightening future" (CMM 121). And these were aggravated by the shocking news of her Aunt Mary Spencer's death in January after a failed, and, she thought, unnecessary operation.

A kind letter from Dwight Morrow made a positive impression on Betty, and for the rest of her senior year they continued to correspond. Unfortunately, the familiarity in letters did not translate to the in-person contact: "His letters are more interesting than he is," she diaried (CMM 130). When an amorous Dwight came for her graduation weekend, she took offense at his advances; they quarreled, and he did not stay for the ceremonies. Betty asked for and received the letters she had written him, then burned them along with the letters he had written to her. All but the last, that is, leaving open the possibility of future correspondence.

One other thing kept the door open. The new Amherst alumnus had published an autobiographical story called "The First Milestone," a tribute to his older sister Agnes, who had been a mentor and inspiration to him. At her engagement, the boy realized that big sister was grown and it was now time to grow up himself. That meant attending college and looking forward to having his own family. "He grew to love another girl," the story reads, "the only girl who had ever reminded him of his sister. He read in her eyes that story, which came to him like a dream out of the past, and he was happy" (DWMFM 18). Betty Cutter realized that she had to be that other girl, and she told Dwight that she wished to see anything else he might write for publication. She closed her letter with these conciliatory words:

Goodbye is such a very final word, I think 'auf wiedersehen' pleasanter, and I am, as ever

Very sincerely your friend,

Elizabeth Reeve Cutter (CMM 136).

3. A Long-Distance Relationship

In retrospect, it is difficult to imagine that the wonderful partnership of Dwight Morrow and Elizabeth Cutter should need another five years to reach engagement, and two more, seven in all, to reach marriage. Their relationship was not only long in years but also in distance, stretching as it did between Cleveland, New York, and Europe before finally getting settled in Massachusetts in 1901. In-person meetings were rare, and once again letters, few though they were initially, bound them together and helped them survive two other apparent in-person breakups.

Just as Morrow after graduation had chafed under the limitations of life back in Pittsburgh before heading to New York and law school, Betty Cutter suffered at home from what her contemporaries referred to as the "first-year-out blues" (CMM 140), today sometimes called post-graduation depression. Rather than wallow in self-pity, however, she determined, "Oh! I must accomplish something…I must do something. I must be something" (CMM 139). Initially, that "something" was of her own creation to support herself, "parlor teaching," giving cultural talks and mini-courses to local social groups and aspiring students. She did have an active social life, and with one of her beaus, an Englishman by the name of William L. Torrance, aimed to enrich the culture of old Cleveland. Accordingly, "they decided that a club, formed to read and discuss the best fiction, should be the intellectual weapon with which they should challenge the mediocrity around them" (RH). On December 15, 1896 a small group met in the Cutter home to found The Classical Novel Reading Union. Soon retitled The Novel Club of Cleveland, the group met monthly to discuss an assigned novel and an accompanying critical paper. Despite some periods of winnowing and falling away, the Club has thrived for well over a century and today has this Internet presence: www. thenovelclub.org.

Betty's desire to broaden her cultural horizons was fulfilled in 1899 when her great-uncle, Dr. John Reeve, took her and sister Annie—later joined by their parents, sister Edith, and Mrs. Cutter's cousin Mary Kissick—on what turned out to be a two-year family vacation *cum* study to Europe. Shortly before the July 13 departure from New York, she met briefly with Dwight Morrow, but once again his strong feelings clashed with her reticence. Fortunately, as she was about to sail, flowers and a long letter from Morrow arrived. Reading it after they were underway, Betty told her sister, "If you ever get a letter like this from a man, you should think a long time before turning him down" (CMM 152), and resolved to continue the correspondence.

Reeve and the Cutter nieces sailed first to England, then traveled to Switzerland and France, where the sisters undertook an intensive study of French. When Reeve returned to the US, the rest of the Cutters arrived. After leaving Paris, they toured Germany, Switzerland again, and Italy, where they spent the winter in Florence, studying and socializing with numerous visiting friends and family members. Frustrated by very mixed results at trying to publish in American magazines, Betty sought a teaching position for the following school year and was pleased to receive a firm offer from her former mentor, Miss Middleberger.

When the Cutters returned from Italy on May 6, 1901, Dwight took Betty to the theater, and once again the in-person meeting foundered. After a long discussion that night and a farewell at the train for Cleveland two days later, both believed that their parting was final. That was to change through a most fortunate "coincidence" that brought them together in July.

Betty took a summer job as companion to her father's invalid cousin, Sarah Cutter, and on July 9 travelled with her to the resort village of Annisquam, Massachusetts, on the water just north of Boston. It so happened that Charles Burnett, Dwight Morrow's closest friend from Amherst and well known to Betty, was also vacationing at the same hotel and had planned to ask Morrow to join him. In light of past disagreements, both men took care to be sure that Betty would not be discomfited by Dwight's presence. Assured that she would not, Morrow arrived on the evening of July 24, then spent two active and stimulating days with her, "the first time in seven years they had more than a few hours together" (CMM 177–8). Assured on July 26 that he would not press his case with her until he knew her better, she replied, "Don't you think you know me well enough now?" (CMM 178). That was the breakthrough, a de facto engagement, what Betty called "a perfect understanding" (CMM 179).

The formal engagement would not come for almost a year and a half. Dwight had targeted the salary he would require to marry and the date when he might attain it. He also did not wish to approach his employer, Mr. Simpson, with personal requests until he had become more established. In the interval, his fierce work ethic established him further in his career and let him grow closer to his beloved with more letters and visits. And "to Betty the great gift of the months of waiting was the confidence with which he infused her, confidence in herself, in him, and in their future together. . . and he never ceased to reassure her nor to proclaim his own infinite faith in her powers" (CMM 187–8).

Betty and Dwight were wed at the Cutter home in Cleveland on Tuesday, June 16, 1903 and honeymooned for a month in New England. The keynote of their storybook life together was sounded in Betty's diary entry of June 21: "D. and I have been married five days and it is as natural as breathing."

4. Married Life

At the tail end of the honeymoon, the Morrows visited the Robert DeForests at their Long Island estate. "It was during those days that she realized how protracted and how solitary, how wise and tentative, must be her endeavor to build up around their mutual devotion a social atmosphere which should both soothe and stimulate her husband's intellectual restlessness; an atmosphere which, while satisfying her own fastidiousness, would entail no lowering of the proud standards of her independence. The contemplation of this responsibility filled her with a sudden seriousness. In the years that followed she was to prove that a perfect marriage can, while remaining an idyll, become an epic" (HN 78).

While living in temporary housing and realizing that they could not afford a suitable home in New York, the Morrows spent an August, 1903 weekend with an old friend, John Kerr, in Englewood, New Jersey and very much liked what they saw. After a short time renting on West Palisade Avenue, they stretched their budget to rent a home at 71 Spring Lane, at the base of the hill that leads up to the Palisades above the Hudson River and only a few blocks' walk from the train station. From there

The Morrows' "little brown house" at 71 Spring Lane Courtesy Englewood Historical Society

Dwight would take the train to Jersey City and then the ferry to lower Manhattan, where his office was located. They moved in, wrote Betty in her diary, on October 28, 1903. "Our moving day! Bought groceries in the morning. Tonight, dear supper in our dining room, Dwight and I, and then a fire in the library! This is home!" In this Englewood home, fondly known as "the little brown house" the Morrows' first three children were born.

As a frustrated college graduate penned up in her parents' home, Betty had lamented that it was not possible to be "historical and social and domestic all at once" (SH 47). Now she faced a similar challenge, but with considerably more success. As constant companion and encourager, an indispensable helpmate and soulmate, she was involved in all stages of Dwight's ascendant career, though one could say she was even more "historical" in the two-plus decades after his passing. She was certainly "domestic" in raising four children and managing the ample assistance from nannies and domestic staff. She actively planned regular family activities such as summer stays at Quogue, an upscale resort village on Long Island's south shore and large rented homes on Cape Cod, as well as winter getaways to the Bahamas. Later, of course, summers were spent at North Haven, Maine, first in rentals, then at the Morrow compound, Deacon Brown's Point.

An avid traveler from her youth, Betty accompanied Dwight on several of his European trips beginning with two visits to England in 1907 and 1908. In 1911 they undertook an extended tour of the European continent with their three children and governess. In 1918, during World War I, they traveled together to the Allied Maritime Transport Council in London and Paris. In

1922 they, along with daughter Constance, Mrs. Annie Cutter, and Mrs. Clara Morrow, visited Dwight's brother, Jay, in Panama where he was Governor of the Canal Zone. Betty returned the next year with Anne, Dwight Jr., and Constance. In other postwar travels, they took their four children on educational tours to England, Scotland, France, and Switzerland. In 1930, with daughter Elisabeth, they sailed to London for the Naval Conference.

In supporting Dwight Morrow's four careers in the 28 years of their marriage, Betty was most certainly "social," a gracious hostess[13] at their frequent business events, an active member of Englewood ladies' societies, member of the National Board of the Y.W.C.A., and, together with Dwight, a benefactor of numerous civic organizations and charities such as Englewood Hospital, Englewood Library, and The Social Service Federation of Englewood, to name but a few. They were also devoted supporters of their alma maters. Dwight, as mentioned earlier, was an active advocate and fundraiser for Amherst College, but he also supported Betty's efforts by publicly pledging to give similar amounts of money to her educational institutions (MEM). Betty served Smith as Alumnae Association president, member of the college's War Services Board for overseas relief, Alumnae Representative to the Board of Trustees, chairman of the 50th Birthday Gift that made possible the completion of the

---

13 At a time when a wife's entertaining was considered so important for the enhancement and success of her husband's career, this anecdote illustrates Betty Morrow's mastery of the art. When the Morrows' friend Pitney van Dusen was president of Union Theological Seminary, his wife, Betty, would ask Betty Morrow to come give the wives of the graduating future ministers a talk on successful entertaining (MEM).

First Presbyterian Church Courtesy Englewood Historical Society

quadrangle, and, in 1926, was named Trustee by the Board. One diary entry illustrates her passion for Smith: "I marched in the Alumnae Parade as I intend to do until I die!" (6/16/27). 1926 also saw the construction and dedication of two lasting memorials to the distinguished alums, Morrow Dormitory at Amherst and Morrow House at Smith.

Both Morrows were also active members of the historic First Presbyterian Church, founded in 1860 as the first Presbyterian congregation in Bergen County and the first church building erected in Englewood. Built around the classic 1870 sanctuary, the church grew over the years until a fire destroyed it in 2016. The Morrows were both raised in devout Presbyterian families, and Betty's diaries show that they maintained their faith through shared Bible study and readings of favorite prayers and Scripture. They raised their children in the faith, at church and with regular family devotions at home and hymn singing in the car on trips. They also had close ties to Union Theological Seminary in New York, which received a sizable gift from Dwight Morrow's will. Mrs. Morrow became the first woman on Union's Board, and the seminary's president would later speak at her funeral.

———

In 1909, after six years in Spring Lane, the Morrows moved up the hill to a more spacious Palisade Avenue home whimsically described by Elisabeth as "a mild example of late gingerbread architecture with fancy trimming around the windows and a little tower over the front door" (HN 110). Anne was most attached to this home, which had a large garden and an ample yard with paths connecting the children to neighboring playmates. While extremely modest compared to the estates of Morrow's prominent friends and colleagues on the East Hill, this house served the Morrows exceedingly well, and they stayed there until December, 1928. Fondly referred to by the family as "The Old House," it was razed in 1930 to allow for the widening of Palisade Avenue.

Even as Englewood remained their primary residence, the Morrows in 1919 invested in an 7,000-square-foot apartment at 4 East 66th Street in Manhattan, at the corner of Fifth Avenue on Central Park East.[14] This move seemed to follow the promptings of Morrow's Morgan partners who had departed Englewood

---

14   Morrow, along with business associates Charles Norton and Cornelius Bliss, commissioned the structure and took the top three apartments. Then they drew lots, and Morrow won the penthouse. It was a great investment for all. Interestingly, the Morrow apartment was eventually owned by Paul Allen of Microsoft. At his death in 2018, it sold for a record price (MEM).

The Morrows' "old house" on East Palisade Avenue Courtesy Englewood Public Library

for the city or Long Island, and indeed it offered access to expanded business, cultural, and social circles. "J. P. Morgan & Co. are making history and we are not in New York to enjoy it," Dwight mused, and Betty added, "The truth is that we have outgrown Englewood and yet cling to it" (HN 227). They did indeed cling to Englewood, to which they returned on weekends after spending the business and school week in the New York, where Anne and Constance attended Miss Chapin's School. The Morrows also maintained friendships developed in their early married life, even as they moved ever higher in the power circles of the big city. "Dwight Morrow and his wife considered it the height of vulgarity to lose contact with early friends," wrote Harold Nicolson. "Throughout his life he was always available for the affairs of his own community" (HN 113).

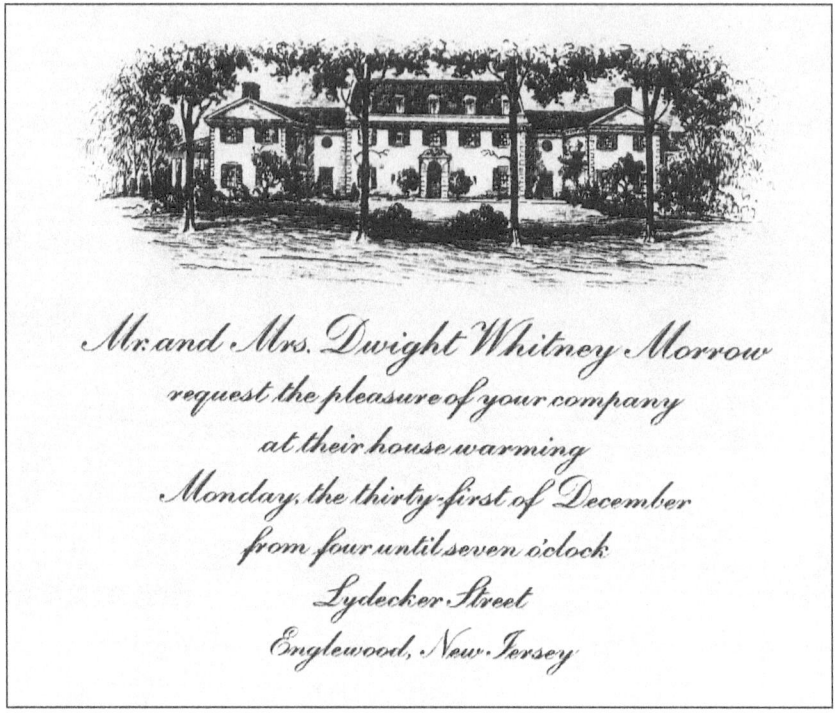

Mr. and Mrs. Dwight Whitney Morrow
request the pleasure of your company
at their house warming
Monday, the thirty-first of December
from four until seven o'clock
Lydecker Street
Englewood, New Jersey

Housewarming invitation to the Morrows' new house on Next Day Hill
Courtesy Englewood Public Library

Dwight would gladly have stayed in the old house, but Betty had her heart set on a custom residence, and she created a beauty.[15] It was inspired by the stately President's House at Smith College and designed by the distinguished architectural firm of Delano and Aldrich, the latter partner being the brother of Betty's close college

---

15   It was not vanity that made Betty Morrow push for a larger house, but the trajectory at that point of Dwight's career as well as her own interests. Many saw him as a presidential hopeful, and security for the family was a concern of his. Busy as Betty was when Dwight was elected senator, she was surprised at how busy senators' wives were expected to be. She needed a New Jersey base of operations that was designed for all the entertaining and meetings that she and her team were going to have to put on. Large numbers of visitors, sometimes without warning (see p. 130), would descend on the Morrow estate (MEM).

friend Amey Aldrich. The three-story brick Georgian Revival structure sat on 52 acres of Englewood's prestigious East Hill. On Lydecker Street north of Palisade Avenue, it was dubbed Next Day Hill, another take-off on the name Morrow, like their Mexican home, Casa Mañana. On December 31, 1928, aided by 20 police officers to manage traffic, the Morrows hosted a house warming for 960 family members, friends, and business associates from far and wide. A Mexican costumed band provided entertainment. In 1936, after Dwight's and daughter Elisabeth's death, and even as Betty continued to reside there, the estate became home to the Elisabeth Morrow School when the Little School moved from Linden Avenue to Lydecker Street.

At the same time as the Morrows commissioned the new Englewood home, they engaged Chester Aldrich to build them a summer home on the island of North Haven, Maine, a one-hour ferry ride from the town of Rockland. Once again, they had followed the lead of Tom Lamont, who in 1917 had purchased there a 100-acre property that he named Sky Farm, and he introduced the island to numerous prominent families who built there as well. Sky Farm has remained in the Lamont family, and most recently it has been used by great-grandson Ned Lamont, governor of Connecticut.

The Morrows' first visit to North Haven was in 1919 with visits to the Nortons and Lamonts. They rented for several summers before purchasing and developing in 1927 84 acres on a bluff above the waters of Penobscot Bay. The home was located on the old farm of Deacon Sam Brown at a spot referred to as Deacon Brown's Point. It featured a beautiful view across to the Camden Hills, a sight wistfully noted by Betty and Anne in their diaries. Finished in 1928, the Aldrich-designed wood frame home—"The Big House"—had 28 rooms and a 1,400-foot waterfront on Grant Cove. There was also a boat house for Lindbergh's 38-foot cabin cruiser, the *Mouette*, and a 21-foot sailboat. A large lawn running alongside the house was first used as a small golf course and then as a short landing strip when Charles and Anne came to visit. A couple of hundred yards away stood "The Little House," a handsome white Cape Cod style cottage that was, at Dwight Morrow's request, designed by a family friend, Lucia Norton Valentine, daughter of Charles and Katherine Norton and a graduate of Columbia University School of Architecture. Built for the Morrow children, it was owned for a time by Constance and is currently owned by her daughter Elisabeth Morgan Pendleton (MEM).

On her 22nd birthday, Anne poetically registered what the summer home meant to her:

The new house!

unbelievably good and right for us— delicious wood smells

white paint

familiar furniture and china

hot water

candles

coming home! (6/22/1928).

For island resident Eleanor Motley Richardson, North Haven stood "for a mental and physical refuge, literally, a safe haven" (121). The idyllic location was certainly that for both the Morrows and Lindberghs, a welcome refuge from the stresses of high-powered business, politics, and celebrity. As in Englewood and New York, the Morrows were active in the community. Dwight was a director of the North Haven Golf Club, while Betty served on the building committee for a new library and was very involved in supporting the church on North Haven. After Mrs. Morrow's death in 1955, the Deacon Brown's Point property was broken up. When renting the Big House proved impracticable, consideration was given to tearing it down. Fortunately, a descendant of Dwight's law partner Thomas D. Thacher purchased the property and beautifully restored it.[16]

What follows is a thumbnail sketch of each of the four young Morrows:

Elisabeth Reeve Morrow (March 17, 1904–December 3, 1934). The Morrows' first-born attended Englewood schools for a while but later boarded at Milton Academy about 10 miles south of Boston. She then attended her mother's alma mater, Smith College, graduating in 1925. After study in France at the Sorbonne and in Grenoble, Elisabeth taught school in Mexico during the time that her father was ambassador. Her success at that venture reinforced her long-held dream to start and direct her own school, which she did in 1930. With the great help of her Smith College friend Constance Chilton, she incorporated The Little School in a white home with a picket fence on East Linden

---

16 A fuller description of the Morrow estate at Deacon Brown's Point, along with personal recollections of the Morrows and Lindberghs by island native Lewis Haskell, is found in the Appendix.

Elisabeth Morrow's "Little School" on East Linden Avenue Courtesy Englewood Historical Society

Avenue in Englewood, beginning with 40 students ranging from 18 months up to five years.

In 1932, suffering from heart disease, Elisabeth left the school, married British diplomat Aubrey Niel Morgan at Next Day Hill, and moved with him to his native Wales. She suffered another heart attack there before travelling to California, where Will Rogers, the family friend who had supported Ambassador Morrow in Mexico, offered the Morgans the use of his ranch. Elisabeth did enjoy a final visit there from the Lindberghs, and her mother was present at her death in Pasadena on December 3, 1934.

A few years after Elisabeth's passing, Betty donated acreage from the Morrow Estate and, with the financial help of the surviving Morrow children, a new Little School was constructed on Lydecker Street. On the present-day Elisabeth Morrow School campus, that structure now houses grades 1–4, while classes for age 2 to kindergarten meet in Chilton House. After Mrs. Morrow's death in 1955, friends and trustees purchased her home from the estate, and the Morrow School, grades 5–8, became the sole tenant of the Morrow House.

Anne Spencer Morrow (June 22, 1906–February 7, 2001). Second-born Anne attended the Dwight School, a private girls' school near her home on Palisade Avenue in Englewood. Her high school work was completed at Miss Chapin's School, a small prep school for girls in Manhattan. Like her mother and sister, Anne attended Smith College, graduating with distinction in 1928. One year later she married the famous aviator Charles Lindbergh, and the couple had six children. Highlights of her married and family life will be presented in Chapter 8.

Dwight Whitney Morrow, Jr. (November 28, 1908–September 4, 1976). Intellectually and athletically gifted, Dwight, Jr. boarded at Groton School, about 40 miles northwest of Boston. Like his father, he attended Amherst College, graduating in 1933, then did graduate work at Harvard and Yale. On various occasions, beginning in his student years, he was plagued by and treated for mental and emotional illness. In 1937 Dwight Jr. married Margot Loines, who became a great friend to the Morrow family. The couple had three children and divorced in 1946. After several years managing a ranch and then a dairy farm in California, he taught international relations, history, and economics at Lincoln University in New York and Temple University in Philadelphia. In 1970 Dwight married Nancy Lofton of Carmel, California, a prominent teacher and administrator, and he taught at the nearby Monterey Institute of Foreign Studies. He died in Monterey at the age of 67.

Constance Cutter Morrow (June 27, 1913–March 25, 1995), was born in Englewood, attended Miss Chapin's School in New York, then boarded at Milton Academy, and, like her mother and sisters, attended Smith College, graduating Phi Beta Kappa and Summa Cum Laude in 1935. In an eerie foreshadowing of her nephew Charlie, in 1929, while still at Milton, she was threatened with kidnapping unless a ransom was paid. A mentally unstable local woman was identified as the letter writer, and because she promised to enter treatment, no charges were pressed (MEM).

In 1937 Con married Aubrey Niel Morgan, the widower of her sister Elisabeth, and then earned an MA in English Literature from Columbia University. In 1939 she and Aubrey were recruited to furnish summaries of events in the American media for the British Press Service and to help give Britain a voice in the United States in case of war. Existing offices were eventually combined under Aubrey's leadership to form the British Information Services.

After the war, the Morgans ran a farm in southwest Washington State, but once again Aubrey was tapped for vital service to Britain, this time as personal assistant and counsellor to the British Ambassador in Washington, DC. After five years they returned to the farm where they raised their four children. Like her mother, Elizabeth, Con continued to render great service to her alma mater, Smith College. For 15 years she served on the Board of Trustees, chairing it for four of those years. In

1978 she published *A Distant Moment: The Youth, Education, & Courtship of Elizabeth Cutter Morrow*, which we extensively cited earlier in this chapter.

⸻

It is interesting to note how several of the Morrow relatives, including Dwight's three sisters, wound up living in and around Englewood. **Agnes Morrow Scandrett**, widowed in 1918, lived first in the Highwood section of north Englewood, then just over the city line in Tenafly. **Alice Morrow**, who never married, lived at 445 Riverside Drive in New York after a teaching career in Constantinople. Her mother, Clara, was also listed at that address, so perhaps the family owned or rented a unit in that apartment building. Later, Alice and Agnes lived in a large home at 71 Franklin Street, a few blocks south of Palisade Avenue. Their

Jay Morrow's home at 71 Franklin Street Courtesy Susan M. Kenney

brother, **General Jay J. Morrow**, and his wife, Harriet, owned the home and resided there.

The third sister, **Hilda Morrow McIlvaine**, and her husband, the **Rev. Dr. Edwin L. McIlvaine**, married in July, 1900, raised their children in western Pennsylvania and moved to Englewood in 1932. They later resided only blocks away at 22 Woodland Park Drive, Tenafly.

From 1933 until his retirement in 1947, Dr. McIlvaine was the Stated Supply pastor at the Community Church on Hudson Avenue, keeping his Presbyterian affiliation while serving the Dutch Reformed congregation. Thereafter he was Honorary Pastor Emeritus until his death in 1962.

Betty Morrow's sister, **Edith Cutter Yates**, her husband **Sheldon Smith Yates**, and their sons **David** and **Rob** also resided in Englewood. Their home at 440 Highview Road was just up the street behind Next Day Hill.

———

The Morrows' prominent neighbors warrant mention here as an illustration of how unique, attractive, and influential Englewood was at that time, "the bedroom of Wall Street" or "Morgan's branch office," as some called it.

Henry P. Davison (1867–1922), co-founder of Bankers Trust and later a J.P. Morgan partner, resided in the mansion he built at 54 Beech Road, just south of Palisade Avenue. He was only casually acquainted with Morrow in Englewood before moving to Long Island in 1909. However, in 1913, as Morgan was seeking another partner, Davison made a point of returning to watch Morrow deliver a speech at the armory on behalf of the Englewood Hospital. He was impressed enough to further make Morrow's acquaintance and recommend him for the position.

Thomas W. Lamont (1870–1948), was hired by Davison at Bankers Trust, then followed him to J. P. Morgan. After first residing on Maple Street, he then purchased Davison's home a few blocks away on Beech Road and was thus a close neighbor to the Morrows. Lamont was well acquainted with the Morrows, for his wife, Florence Corliss, an Englewood native, had been a classmate of Betty's at Smith College. Lamont started with Bankers Trust and was, with Davison, instrumental in bringing Morrow to Morgan, where they served together until Morrow's departure for diplomacy in Mexico in 1927. Lamont left a significant footprint of benevolence in academe—the Lamont Library at Harvard College, his alma mater, where he served as trustee, and Columbia University's Lamont–Doherty Earth Observatory. The LDEO is housed at the Lamonts' weekend estate in Palisades, New York, overlooking the Hudson River and only 15–20 minutes' drive north of Englewood. It was donated to Columbia by Mrs. Lamont after her husband's death. The Lamonts lie buried near the Morrows in Brookside Cemetery.

Seward Prosser (1871–1942) was board president of Bankers Trust in New York, second only in size to J. P. Morgan. He was director on the boards of many other leading firms and renowned for raising millions for Englewood Hospital, the Red Cross, and other relief organizations. After attending the Englewood School for Boys, Prosser had remained in town, where he and his wife,

Constance, lived first on Engle Street and then at 47 Beech Road. At both homes they were friends and close neighbors to the Morrows' Spring Lane and Palisade Avenue residences. Prosser died at his Woods Hole, Massachusetts home, but he too is buried in Brookside Cemetery.

Daniel E. Pomeroy was an officer and director at Bankers Trust, active in New Jersey politics, twice vice chairman of the Republican National Committee, and in1928 eastern campaign manager for Herbert Hoover. It was he who first contacted Dwight Morrow about leaving Mexico to run for Senator from New Jersey. Pomeroy and his wife, Frances, lived at 41 Beech Road.

Harlan F. Stone, Morrow's Amherst classmate, practiced law and served as dean of Columbia Law School in New York. Before he was nominated by classmate Calvin Coolidge to the Supreme Court, where he became chief justice, he lived at 2 Chestnut Street.

Elizabeth Morrow's diaries from 1927 to 1931 afford us a delightful behind-the-scenes look at the culmination of Dwight's brilliant career, the ambassadorship to Mexico, as well as insights into the problematic, abbreviated Senate term. Recalling Betty's earlier comment about the impossibility of being "historical and social and domestic all at once," we find that she once again manages the domestic life of the family and the social aspects as teammate in the historic efforts of her husband, a graceful *Embajadora* (ambassador's wife) hosting large groups at the Embassy. This section will mention a few of the recurring themes in her diaries

Englewood welcomes the Morrows home from the London Naval Conference, April 29, 1930 Courtesy Amherst College Archives and Special Collections

that flesh out the Dwight Morrow chronology presented in Chapters 5 and 6 and grant us an intimate look into the life and era of this most remarkable woman.

As we have seen before, Betty Morrow's ties to Englewood and her homes there were powerful and heartfelt. Though she had just built her dream house on Next Day Hill, she was still able to say about the Palisade Avenue home, "Last night in old house. I know I can never love another so much" (9/13/28). Several times after her trips to Mexico and to Europe, she would enter something along these lines, "Home again! Oh! How heavenly it is to be here!" (4/9/30). Dwight returned from London on a later ship, and after a nice New York reception, Englewood turned out in style to cheer him: "The streets were lined with children waving flags and flowers. It was a great welcome home" (4/29/30).

The fact is, Betty was a very adaptable and happy person who fit in anywhere. Greeted by a welcoming crowd to begin her second year in Mexico, she spoke of "a warm comfortable at-home feeling" (9/18/28) in the city and her affection for the weekend home in "Beloved Cuernavaca!" (9/16/30). Another Morrow word play referred to her Maine getaway: "I am really here and could write 'North *Heaven.*' I'm so happy" (8/3/30). Still, Englewood remained the true "home" of her heart.

Betty was a prolific letter writer and regularly kept in touch with both family and friends, several of whom came to visit in Mexico. Most of all she was concerned to keep the family intact amidst the pressures of geographical separation, diplomatic obligations, and the ongoing health concerns of Elisabeth and Dwight, Jr. By the fall of 1928, after the heady first year of welcomes, Christmas togetherness, the Lindbergh visit, and diplomatic breakthroughs, both Betty and Dwight were "homesick for our children" (10/8/28). This was remedied some when the Morrows reunited for the move to Next Day Hill just before Christmas, 1928: "All the children are sleeping under the new roof tonight!" (12/20/28). The mother hen also noted satisfaction at another significant reunion: "Married 27 years today and tonight all the children are at home!" (6/16/30).

Typical of Betty's close relationship to her "precious girls" (1/17/29) was a diary entry about the youngest, Constance, who was still in the nest: "I've just had a lovely talk and snuggle with Con and tucked her into bed" (9/1/28). But after Anne's sensational engagement and marriage to Charles Lindbergh— Betty called the latter "that day of terrible excitement" (5/27/30)—

it was Betty's second-born who most evoked the diarist's emotional highs and lows. Initially, her concerns were for the couple's compatibility: "Anne is engaged to Colonel Lindbergh! I think that I can never be surprised again. I am stunned. . . . He's so utterly different from her. . . . They have only met four times since last Christmas" (11/11/28). Betty often testifies to missing the first married-off child—"How I long for Anne!" (4/9/30)— and feeling elated when she hears from her: "My heart is like a singing bird. I have been singing with joy all day" (7/18/29).

Later, she understandably records apprehension for the couple's safety as pioneering aviators. For example, at London's Buckingham Palace, "Both the King and Queen received us. He stopped Dwight in line to ask about Anne's flying and if we felt perfectly comfortable about it. Dwight said, 'No—we do not'" (3/25/30). With the Morrow offspring moving into adulthood and their parents still traveling regularly, Betty acknowledged a significant family transition that is worth documenting at length.

"Last night I could not sleep. I was thinking of Anne, and the break-up in our life with the children no longer close about us, and the moving to Washington, and the whole upheaval. It seemed too terrible. I suppose this is the last phase. You need courage to bring children into the world, and then courage to let them go away to school, and then to see them married and to learn to live without them. Every now and then I have these moments of losing Anne again and it is overwhelming" (3/31/30).

Still, even with the anxiety for their safety, there was great joy each time the Lindberghs returned from a hazardous journey, such as after a grueling, record-breaking, cross-country flight in

April, 1930 while Anne was pregnant with her first child: "My precious—my precious Anne is here!. . . . Oh! Anne's home—how wonderful it is!" (4/20/30).

Betty Morrow's activities outside of diplomatic and familial matters are also recorded in her diary, often with gentle, self-deprecating humor. She and the ambassador both took language lessons, but, she claimed, with little success on her part. "My Spanish lessons are a farce" (11/20/28), she lamented. "I make no progress in Spanish. I don't study" (11/4/29). Still, after a White House dinner in honor of Mexican president-elect Ortiz Rubio, she conceded, "Never has my sputtering Spanish been more useful" (12/28/29).

There are sporting entries as well, such as watching the great Bill Tilden play tennis, swimming, and playing golf three times a week, again with varying success. "Golf this morning. It is disgusting the way I play," followed by "I made my best score—52" (1/17/29).

Most of all, it was Betty Morrow's involvement with the arts and culture in Mexico that distinguished her non-professional activity. As mentioned in Chapter 5, she and her husband patronized excellent local craftsmen and artists as they outfitted their home in Cuernavaca. They also commissioned the renowned Mexican artist Diego Rivera to create in the Palacio de Cortés an impressive mural titled *History of Morelos, Conquest and Revolution*. The frescoes depict the history of the state of Morelos from the early-16th-century Spanish conquest up to the Mexican Revolution of 1910. They remain today a source of local pride and, with the palace itself, a top tourist attraction.

At the same time, Betty was developing her literary talents. She was proud to have a poem published in the 1929 edition of *The Winged Horse Anthology* and another accepted by *Harper's Magazine* the following year. She also created a delightful children's book called *The Painted Pig: A Mexican Picture Book* (1930). The highly successful book, which stayed in print over 30 years, was inspired by a pottery piggy bank painted with Mexican designs that she, with daughter Constance, to whom the book is dedicated, had bought at a market. The book tells of two children, Pita and Pedro, trying to coax a toy maker into producing a second piggy bank, so each child can have one. The colorful pictures were by René d'Harnoncourt, an Austrian artist who collaborated with Betty on a second book, *Bird, Beast and Fish: An Animal Alphabet* (1933).[17] He also spent some time with the Morrows helping them decorate their new Englewood home with a Mexican-themed tile wall. After several diary mentions of the book's conception, contract, and rewriting, she reported on September 5, 1930, "And *The Painted Pig* is here—10 copies!" Only three weeks later, she was pleased to report, "The first edition is sold out" (9/30/30). The following year, Betty Morrow published a collection of her poetry called *Quatrains for My Daughter*.

In Dwight Morrow's final nine months of service as ambassador, Betty supported him in two major undertakings outside of Mexico, which she entertainingly recorded in her diary: the London Naval Conference and the US Senate Campaign. She and daughter Elisabeth accompanied Morrow to London in

---

17   Interestingly, René's brother, Nicholas, a prominent author and conductor, composed a musical accompaniment to the book (MEM).

January, 1930, though the ladies also spent two weeks in Paris. One has to think that her presence was a great encouragement to him as he labored to craft an agreement between the skittish participants who often threatened to pull out of the negotiations. She would also have been a gracious partner in the many social events that brought them in touch with several luminaries of the time.

Will Rogers, a good friend of the family who spent time with them in Mexico, Englewood, and later in California, also saw them in the first days of the conference. On various occasions at the royal residence in Buckingham Palace and the prime minister's residence at 10 Downing Street, the Morrows met, in addition to the king and queen, four British politicians who were or would become prime minister: Lloyd George, Stanley Baldwin, Ramsay McDonald, and Winston Churchill. Lunch with the famed Irish playwright George Bernard Shaw elicited this diary entry: "G. B. S. was most approachable and easy to talk to, especially about his latest play, but he didn't thrill me much" (2/2/30). While in England, Betty was approached by the Girl Scouts of America and asked to take their presidency, an honor that she turned down. Elisabeth, for her part, about to start her own school in Englewood, spent a stimulating day at the experimental Beacon Hill School, founded by the renowned British intellectual Bertrand Russell. Betty lunched with and was impressed by Sidney and Beatrice Potter Webb, leading British economists, members of the socialist Fabian Society, and co-founders of the London School of Economics.

It was on this trip that the Morrows also got to know the British politician, diplomat, and author Harold Nicolson, who, of course, was later commissioned by Betty to write the biography of Dwight. Nicolson also placed his English home at the Lindberghs' disposal when in December, 1935, concerned for the safety of their second son, Jon, after the kidnapping and murder of Charles, Jr., they fled to Europe to escape the oppressive media and public scrutiny that harassed them in the US.

The other prominent role that Betty Morrow played at the end of her husband's career was as energetic campaigner in his bid for the Senate. She was happy to do it but admitted that the campaign trail could be strenuous. After a New Year's Day reception at the Englewood Armory, she wrote, "my hand still aching from the vigorous handshakes of Bergen County" (1/2/30). And while she confessed to being "sick of dinners" (5/6/30), overall she gives the impression of a happy warrior who believes in her cause and nimbly adapts to the needs of the moment. "I'm 57 today," she wrote on her birthday, "and still going strong" (5/29/30).

By June 7, ten days before the primary, Betty had appeared in 16 of New Jersey's 21 counties, mostly giving speeches to and socializing with large women's groups—450 ladies in Ridgewood and the same number in Essex County. A meeting at the Republican headquarters in Trenton had 350 in attendance with "screaming speeches about Dwight as a paragon of virtue, George Washington and Abraham Lincoln mixed!" (5/8/30). A week later, May 15, came Morrow's signature speech calling for the repeal of prohibition. "It was splendid; a clear, dignified, reasoned statement as to his belief. The crowd went wild and the press is already saying it is the most important statement since

Hoover's speech of acceptance" (5/15/30). Many telegrams of congratulation were received, though Betty was called upon to address one group not so pleased by the address. On May 23rd she traveled to Sussex County in northwest New Jersey and "talked to W.C.T.U. [Women's Christian Temperance Union] women who fear Dwight is allied with the Demon Rum!" (5/23/30).

Betty Morrow also delivered formal radio addresses and, doing retail politics on a grand scale, graciously hosted a staggering number of people—both the general public and the news media—at her home on Next Day Hill. When 30 reporters appeared one day, "We gave them cigars, sandwiches and grape juice. Men were coming and going all day" (5/24/30). A week later, her improvisational skills again came to the fore. "More than 1,500 people came from the northern part of Bergen County to call upon us. We only knew at 2 p.m. that they were coming at 4. I telephoned the Englewood Club and got ginger ale and cookies for them. It was the best we could do on Sunday. They swarmed over the lawn and gardens and seemed to enjoy it all very much" (6/1/30). That number was exceeded two weeks later. "Such a day! This afternoon we have had 1,800 people here, veterans and Gold Star mothers of New Jersey" (6/15/30).

Betty's hard work and personal charm paid great dividends as Dwight Morrow won a landslide victory in the primary, including overwhelming support from his neighbors. "Dwight is most pleased over Englewood's splendid vote for him. . . . He has beaten Fort and Freylinghuysen 2 to 1 in their own districts. The Englewood vote was over 92% for him and his own ward 96½%. Fine editorials in the night's papers" (6/17–6/18/30).

Only days after the primary and for the rest of the summer, Betty's attention would turn back to her family, as documented by Scott Berg: "Next Day Hill practically became a sanitarium, what with doctors checking on Dwight Jr. and on Elisabeth who, in the excitement of opening The Little School, had suffered a mild heart attack" (ASB 216). But the big news for the public, and the press that camped around the Morrow estate, was the arrival of Betty's first grandchild. "Anne has a son!" she wrote on June 22, Anne's 26th birthday, after eleven hard hours of labor attended by a nurse and three doctors. Dwight Morrow's secretary, Arthur Springer, made a brief statement to the press about the birth of a son, but the child's name was not known until Lindbergh called a press conference in New York to announce that it would be Charles Augustus Lindbergh, Jr. Playing off the father's nicknames of "Lucky Lindy" and "The Lone Eagle," newspapers referred to the son as "Wee Lindy" or "Eaglet." An adoring public sent all manner of tributes, gifts, and congratulatory messages to Next Day Hill. Not long after that, the Lindberghs rented an old farmhouse near Princeton, New Jersey and began a search for property of their own, settling on 425 remote acres in the Sourland Mountains a bit farther north. They then engaged the Morrows' architect, Chester Aldrich, to build their dream home in East Amwell Township near Hopewell.

Dwight Morrow returned to his post in Mexico shortly after the birth of his grandson, but Betty stayed behind, concerned for the health of her daughters. Anne, still recuperating from childbirth, had a breast abscess that needed lancing, and Elisabeth had suffered another heart attack on July 24, this time in North

Haven, where she was vacationing with brother Dwight and sister Con. On August 3, Betty was finally able to join them for some family time at North Haven before returning to Mexico on August 18 for the last few weeks of Dwight's tenure as Ambassador. A highlight for the Morrows in those days was the completion of the extensive Diego Rivera murals that they had commissioned to show their respect for Mexican history and folk art.

On September 29, while Dwight was in Washington formally resigning his post with the President, Betty returned to Englewood in time to witness the opening of Elisabeth's school on the 30th. The couple then turned their attention to the general election of November 4, where Morrow comfortably won *twice*—with a 20% margin of victory—first against one Democratic opponent to fill out the remaining months of David Baird's unexpired term and then against another to begin the full six-year Senate term commencing on March 4, 1931. Betty, meanwhile, was announced by the DC press with this society page headline: "Washington Society Looks Forward To Advent of Mrs. Morrow, Wife of U. S. Ambassador To Mexico, As Hostess."

———

Early in what would be the final year of his life, Dwight Morrow proclaimed it "1931, a year for courage!" It was indeed, especially for Betty, whose 28-year marriage ended with the sudden passing of her husband on October 5. Up to then, her schedule for the year reminds us of her earlier thought of being "historical and social and domestic all at once."

The Morrows first lived at the elegant, new Shoreham Hotel and then, after several fruitless real estate searches, eventually established residence in the Georgetown neighborhood of Washington, DC. When in Washington, she and Dwight attended receptions and dinners with numerous dignitaries, including President Hoover, Secretary of State Stimson, Secretary of the Treasury Mellon, numerous Senators, and foreign visitors. Hoover and Stimson in particular, as noted in Chapter 6, relied on Morrow for counsel on economic and international affairs. While Dwight was busy with Senate business, stag events, or Republican functions, Betty frequently attended gatherings of the Ladies of the Senate and functions at the Congressional Club.

The fact is, though, that they were apart or both absent from Washington as much or more than they were there together. Betty's diary chronicles her frequent trips—sometimes for just a few days—back to Englewood and Princeton to check on Elisabeth, Anne, and the baby; to Cleveland to see her family; to Boston to visit daughter Constance; to Northampton, Amherst, and, of course, North Haven. In June she attended *four* commencements in succession at Milton Academy, where Con graduated cum laude and Dwight "made a fine speech—easy witty—w. a touch of wisdom in it as always" (6/12/31); Smith; Amherst, where Dwight received "a perfectly marvelous citation" as he received an honorary doctorate; and Bowdoin College in Brunswick, Maine, where Dwight received yet another honorary doctorate, and when the hood was put over Dwight's head, "that brought the lump into my throat" (6/18/31).

One extended absence from Washington, with Betty's dear friend Amey Aldrich accompanying them, was a planned sightseeing tour to Italy, departing New York on March 11 on the *SS Leviathan*. At the urging of Secretary of State Stimson, they interrupted their trip in London for Dwight to meet with embassy officials, British Prime Minister Macdonald, friends, and colleagues from the 1930 Naval Conference, and to help mediate a naval dispute between France and Italy. After five days, they resumed their travels, arriving in Naples on March 23.

Their trip proceeded south to Sicily staying at grand hotels and focusing on splendid cultural and historical sites such as Greek and Roman temples and amphitheaters, cathedrals, and museums. The occasional arrival of mail from home was, wrote Betty, "The great event of the day" (4/1/31). From Sicily the travelers made their way back north through Naples, Rome, Florence, and Siena to Paris and London.

Departure for home was on April 29 on the *RMS Majestic* and arrival May 5, but along the way "a rapturous cable" (5/3/31) arrived from Elisabeth announcing that she was engaged to a widowed Presbyterian minister named Clyde Roddy. What should have been good news caused extreme anguish for the Morrows, who immediately saw him as a bad match for their daughter. They sought the counsel of family and trusted friends and weighed their own harsh assessment of his character against the "guarded praise" of Roddy's parishioners and associates. After one month of visits from the would-be son-in-law, Betty confessed, "I feel utterly discouraged" (6/8/31), but a month later she exulted, "Thank God! Elisabeth has just told me that she does not expect to marry Clyde" (7/5/31).

Even as she stayed active in local affairs—giving a garden party for Englewood's teachers and attending the Dwight School

Aerial view of the Morrow estate, with Lindbergh's plane, at Deacon Brown's Point, North Haven Courtesy of the North Haven Historical Society, North Haven, Maine

commencement—Betty continued to write for publication and was pleased to have an article on Cuernavaca accepted by *The American Mercury* magazine and to have some of her poems submitted to Alfred Knopf. Knopf also requested more articles about Mexico, which would eventually lead to the publication of *Casa Mañana* in 1932. The sketches for that book were done by Bill Spratling, a silver designer and artist whose work the Morrows had patronized and promoted in Mexico. Betty also engaged René d'Harnoncourt, another collaborator in Mexico— he had created the illustrations for *The Painted Pig*— to install a corridor full of Mexican tiles at Next Day Hill.

In mid-July Betty learned that Anne and Charles' pioneering survey flight to Japan and China was imminent: "Oh! What a thrill of terror it sends through me!" (7/18/31). The Lindberghs

The Lindberghs' plane at North Haven, Maine before their 1931 trip to the Orient
Courtesy of the North Haven Historical Society, North Haven, Maine

did not plan to return until November, and Betty would have the baby, so bonding with her grandson and following Anne's trip in the media became the central events of her active summer on North Haven. She and Anne were both thrilled that it was possible to stop in Maine for a final goodbye. The plane landed before a throng of spectators and was guarded overnight in the Fox Island Thoroughfare between Vinalhaven and North Haven. The takeoff on Thursday, July 30, was another "day of terrific excitement" (7/30/31). After a picnic lunch on the *Mouette*, the Morrows moved down the Thoroughfare to see the plane "skimming over the water, the propeller gleaming in the sun. The plane passed us – they waved & then at the last red buoy they turned – rose – flew over the pine trees and were gone" (7/30/31). Betty charted the many stops on the bold trip, rejoicing each time she received some word via news reports, telegram, radio ("7,000 miles"), even movie newsreels. Anne would later document the voyage in her 1935 book *North to the Orient*.

Except for a couple of brief trips to Englewood, Betty stayed the rest of the summer at Deacon Brown's Point, attending to little Charlie and hosting numerous family members and distinguished visitors such as archeologist Leonard Woolley, poet William Griffith, and Smith president William A. Neilson. Longtime friends, neighbors, and colleagues the Lamonts, Lippmanns, and Nortons were often dinner companions who joined the Morrows for bridge and anagrams. Betty liked to swim and golf, the latter often with Englewood professional Jack Hobens. Despite his lessons, she consistently complained about the poor quality of her game. Dwight Morrow did spend a fair amount of time at North Haven, but he was also absent at times to attend to Senate business. A week after Dwight's frightening vascular spasm on September 10, Betty returned to Englewood while Dwight first went to Boston. They celebrated a photo of Anne's victorious arrival in Tokyo, headlined as "The First Woman to Fly the Pacific!" (9/20/31), and a few days later Betty was thrilled to see Anne in the movies: "I saw Anne! Oh! What a strange thing it is!" (9/24/31). A subsequent report of an accident in China with damage to the Lindberghs' plane caused great concern, but for Betty, the worst was soon to follow when Dwight Morrow died on October 5, 1931.

Beyond the flood of letters and telegrams of tribute and condolence—including from President Hoover, Secretary of State Stimson, and British Prime Minister MacDonald—two honors came hard on the heels of Morrow's death. The day after the funeral, New Jersey's governor asked to appoint Mrs. Morrow to her husband's seat in the US Senate, an offer she declined. A month later, an Englewood town meeting, "full of love for him & the desire to honor him" (11/7/31), voted to name the planned new high school and the surrounding 37-acre park for Dwight Morrow. In a ceremony to begin construction on November 23, Betty applied mortar to the first brick and helped daughters Anne and Elisabeth lay the cornerstone of Dwight Morrow High School (BB-G 81).

December saw Betty acquire a different apartment in New York, at 2 E. 72nd Street, replacing the one on E. 66th Street. Her letter writing continued apace as she acknowledged the many condolences that flowed in after Dwight's death. Finally, on

December 20, she wrote with relief, "I answered the last letter tonight."

Earlier in the year, Dwight Morrow had said, "1931, a year for courage!" His widow recalled that comment in November: "What a terrible meaning those words have for me now!" (11/7/31). And she reflected on them in her final diary entry of the year: "Oh! A new year without Dwight! I go and sit in his chair every night to get courage" (12/31/31).

5. Life After Dwight

The rest of this chapter on Elizabeth Cutter Morrow will briefly present several highlights from the rest of her life as widow, matriarch, educator, activist, and distinguished first lady of Englewood. As mentioned earlier, there is material enough for a full biography of Betty Morrow, but that is for another time and author.

Dwight Morrow's words about courage would equally apply to **1932**, when on March 1 the family's first grandchild, Charles A. Lindbergh, Jr. was kidnapped from Highfields, the Lindberghs' new home in Hunterdon County, New Jersey, and murdered. The event is well known, but Betty's diary gives us her perspective on the second family tragedy within six months. The diary recounts the progress of the case from the ransom letters with the strange signature—three holes, a red circle, and a black one—the command post established by the New Jersey State Police at the Lindbergh home, and the many assurances that the baby was safe and healthy, through the negotiations of Dr. John F. Condon, the intermediary agreed upon by both sides. Condon, known as Jafsie (from his initials JFC), communicated through classified ads posted in the *New York American* newspaper, and Betty Morrow had pasted those ads into her diary. Condon claimed to have had two meetings with one of the kidnappers, whom he named Cemetery John.

There were a great many fruitless "tips" and fraudulent claims, which, along with the waiting, caused constant tension for the family: "For a week we have lived in hell" (3/8/32). Betty's comments reflect her grief as grandmother recalling sweet times with her grandson, as protective mother worrying about her daughter—"The delay for Anne is terrible. . . Oh! My heart aches for her" (3/18)—and as widow, still mourning her recent loss. Words such as "We are trembling with excitement tonight" (3/31) are followed by "Delay again" (4/1). On April 2, she reports, "$70,000.00 [$50,000 actually] has been handed over to the kidnappers tonight. . . Now we can only wait & pray that the kidnappers keep their word" (4/2).

Of course, they did not. The cycle of shock, hope, and disappointment was repeated throughout the ten weeks between the kidnapping and the discovery of the child's body on May 12. He had died of a blow to the head and been left in the woods a few miles from the Lindbergh home.

While the frantic, and thus far fruitless, search for the kidnappers continued, Betty Morrow did enjoy two events in **1933**. First came the formal dedication of the recently completed Dwight Morrow High School. With several state and local dignitaries in attendance, she accepted the ceremonial keys to the school that would forever honor her husband's memory as Englewood's leading citizen.

Then she received an honorary degree from Dwight's alma mater, Amherst College, the first of six such honors.

In September, **1934** there was finally a break in the Lindbergh kidnapping case. A German immigrant named Bruno Richard Hauptmann was arrested after passing a $10 gold certificate from the ransom money and then being found to have over $13,000 more hidden in his garage in the Bronx, New York. In October a grand jury in Flemington, New Jersey indicted Hauptmann for murder, after which he was extradited from New York and placed in a small jail cell at the Hunterdon County Court House.

On December 3, Elizabeth Morrow endured the third profound loss in three years when her eldest daughter, Elisabeth Reeve Morrow Morgan, died in Pasadena, California. Elisabeth, who had founded the Englewood school now bearing her name, had been weakened by a damaged heart for some time and now pneumonia. As Harold Nicolson watched Betty, a reluctant air traveler, leave Englewood to fly through bad weather to be present at her daughter's passing, he recorded a great tribute to the extraordinary character of Elizabeth Morrow: "So small and pathetic she looked. But what guts that woman has got! She is the real pioneer type. I confess that I was deeply impressed" (HND 190).

On January 2, **1935**, the Hauptmann trial began at the court house in Flemington amidst thousands of reporters, media people, security police, and curiosity seekers. Mrs. Morrow was not involved in the trial, though her daughter Anne and son-in-law Charles were called as witnesses for the prosecution. After a six-week trial, Hauptmann was found guilty and sentenced to die in the electric chair, which happened in April the following year.

A second honorary degree came Betty's way this year, from the New Jersey College for Women (NJC) in New Brunswick. Renamed Douglass College in 1955, NJC was the women's college of Rutgers University, which until 1970 was all male.

In **1937**, Betty Morrow received yet another honorary degree, Doctor of Humane Letters, from her alma mater, Smith College. In conferring the degree, President William Allan Neilsen described her with these words: "President of the Alumnae Association, and for sixteen years Trustee of Smith College, author of distinction in prose and verse, the multitude of whose services to her college and her country—far greater than the world knows—makes it impossible to describe adequately the alumna who has earned in most abundant measure our love, our honor, and our gratitude."

It was a busy summer for Betty, who also married off her two youngest children. Constance wed her sister Elisabeth's widower, Aubrey Niel Morgan, and Dwight, Jr. married Margot Loines.

When William Neilson retired as president of Smith College, Betty was appointed as acting president, the first woman to hold that position. She served for the academic year **1939-40**, and, remaining active as a loyal alumna, helped raise the college's endowment from $2 million to $6 million (BB-G 116). Much later she would serve as Honorary Chairman of the 75th Anniversary Fund and endow a lectureship at Smith.

War was raging in Europe in **1940**, with Nazi Germany overrunning Norway, Denmark, France, Belgium, and the Netherlands, leaving Great Britain to defend herself alone. Many in the United States believed that we needed to aid the

British and considered it likely that we would eventually have to fight Germany ourselves. The isolationist group America First wanted no American involvement in the European war, and its most prominent spokesman was Charles Lindbergh, Elizabeth Morrow's son-in-law.

A group taking the opposite position was the Committee to Defend America by Aiding the Allies, based in New York and chaired by the prolific author, editor, and politician William Allen White. Betty Morrow shared the ideals of the Committee, and, on June 4, despite the extreme discomfort of publicly opposing her son-in-law, she delivered an eloquent address on NBC Radio asking the question, "Does America Deserve a Miracle?"

She did not endorse American military involvement in the war; rather, she said, "as the best means of avoiding this type of involvement in the conflict in Europe, I urge immediate aid to the Allies—the sending of munitions and supplies, food, money, airplanes, ships, and everything that could help them win in their struggle against Germany." Though believing in the power of prayer, Betty cited biblical examples that show "a miracle is not a one-sided effort. . . . People earn their miracles." "Does America deserve a miracle?" she asked. "Not unless she earns it."

After the radio broadcast, Betty repeated the speech for the cameras of Pathé News. "Oh! These movie people," she wrote. "How funny they are! Their supreme praise is, 'You would do well in the movies!'" (6/4/40). The speech generated immediate reaction: "All day telegrams & letters have come. . . . Most of them approve – some are terrible in their criticism" (6/7/40).

She answered many of them, which were about three to one in favor of her position. Most newspapers gave her good reviews, "The *Tribune* alas! Calling it a rebuttal to Charles – but A. & C. understand" (6/5/40).

The summer of 1940 brought a flurry of academic honors, first from New York University on June 5 before a crowd of 20,000 on the University Heights campus. The citation introducing her lauded Dwight's service in Mexico and her "maternal genius throughout in an eminent household." Joining her on the platform was the noted American poet Carl Sandburg, "a great American. He was very friendly and sent special messages to Anne" (6/5/40). Interestingly, Sandburg was also present two days later when Betty received an honorary Doctor of Laws degree and gave a six-minute luncheon talk at Lafayette College. A third honorary degree that week was presented on June 11 at Princeton University, with daughter Con and daughter-in-law Margot sitting in front seats.

In her capacity as acting president, Betty presided at the Smith College commencement, after protesting to her diary about "the commencement procedure wh. has completely mixed me up!" and struggling over the citations (6/12/40).

The June 24, **1941** commencement at Dwight Morrow High School marked ten years since Morrow's death and the naming of the school and park in his honor. "Preaching Dwight's internationalism," Mrs. Morrow delivered the commencement address to an "immense crowd" and a class of 308 graduates who would soon see their country enter World War II. At least one member of that class, Burt Wyman, would perish in the conflict.

Betty's talk on "What It Means to Be Educated" challenged the graduates to have a sense of proportion, practice tolerance, and to become "internationally minded, so that when arbitration becomes the mode again our people may have the international view." She may have been referring both to her late husband and to the war clouds on the horizon when she cited "one test of a great man: the willingness to work knowing he will not live to the final victory."

On September 21, **1943**, Betty and her sister-in-law Agnes M. Scandrett christened the Liberty Ship *SS Dwight W. Morrow* at its launch at the St. Johns River Shipbuilding Company, Jacksonville, Florida.

Elizabeth Morrow's **writing career**, which began in Mexico with *The Painted Pig*, individual published poems, and the collection *Quatrains for My Daughter,* continued in her years as a widow with children's books *Beast, Bird and Fish* (1933) and the Tucker Family series. In 1939 she published *A Pint of Judgment: A Christmas Story*, about a child's desire to find just the right gift for her mother. *The Rabbit's Nest* (1940) described the Tucker children learning about what is in a rabbit's nest. That was followed by *Shannon* (1941), the title character being Derek Tucker's Irish terrier.

Betty's **love of and care for family** defined her for the rest of her life. She was mother of the four accomplished adult children introduced above, then beloved grandmother known as "Grandma Bee" to her 13 grandchildren: Anne's six, Dwight Jr.'s three, and Constance's four. The youngest, Eiluned Morgan, surely spoke for all when she said, "I think what was extraordinary

Liberty Ship SS Dwight W. Morrow US Maritime Commission Photo 3777A,
Courtesy Marshall University Special Collections Department, Huntington, WV

about her was how safe and confident a very young child of four or under felt around her. I felt completely loved and cared for. And I loved her world. She made a real effort to see me on my own each visit, both in Englewood and in Mexico. My memories are that we shared our love of gardens. We would plan out our ideal gardens."

The **Christian commitment** that Betty Morrow shared with her husband continued throughout her life. Here are a few examples.

On October 26, 1938 Betty gave a powerful talk to the Englewood Church Women's Society that she called "The Lengthening Shadow." She based the remarks on her trip abroad to London, Paris, and Rome when the infamous Adolf Hitler and Benito Mussolini were casting a sinister "shadow" over Europe. Fortunately, she said, "We do not live in this shadow. . . . We breathe the air of freedom."

On October 6, 1941 in New York City, Betty Morrow addressed a conference on "The Place of Church Women in the Emergency." Entitled "Our Spiritual Heritage," her talk closed with the charge, "Never take your church for granted. People you never knew broke their hearts to get it for you."

On May 22, 1942 continuing her leadership in church affairs, Betty delivered a stirring talk at a church of her youth, Calvary, in Cleveland. She cited the four churches that had meant most to her: the Old Stone Church and Calvary Church in Cleveland, the Union Church of Mexico City, and the First Presbyterian Church in Englewood. "The church was not a *part* of our life," she said, "it *was* our life" (her emphasis). Further, "The gifts brought by

Elizabeth Morrow, Founder, with other Community Chest Leaders
Courtesy Englewood Community Chest

the churches into the political life and social life of our country have never been fully recognized." As examples she cited the Anglican or Episcopal sense of authority, tradition, and beauty; the Methodist hymnbook; and the Baptists' separation of church and state.

The Morrows had long been supporters of New York's Union Theological Seminary, and Betty became the first female member of the Seminary Board.

At Englewood's First Presbyterian Church, she served as the first woman trustee and elder. There she also delivered a talk on "A Mexican Christmas," recalling with gratitude the church's prayers for her and Dwight as they embraced the great challenge of the ambassadorship to Mexico.

We have already referred to Betty Morrow's **involvement in community affairs**, not only in support but also in the actual operation of the worthy causes. These samples should suffice to illustrate her strong commitment to civic engagement:

- Founder and "Honorary Chairman for Life" of the Community Chest in Englewood.
- Council on Foreign Relations.
- Co-founder with Harold Weston of Food for Freedom, Inc.
- Board Member and Honorary Chairman of the Community Service Society.
- Association for Improving the Condition of the Poor.
- Englewood Hospital.
- Executive committee of the New York National War Fund Committee.
- Head of Englewood's City Planning Commission.
- Chairman of the Board of The Little School and commencement speaker at The Elisabeth Morrow School.
- Life Member of The Woman's Club of Englewood.
- Member of the National Board of the YWCA.

Many of these charitable organizations were generously remembered in her will, as were, not surprisingly, Smith and Amherst.

Near the end of 1954, Elizabeth Morrow suffered a stroke at her home. She died on **Sunday, January 23, 1955.** In the press, she was hailed as an "Englewood Benefactor Mourned By The World" and as a marvelously talented poet, educator, and humanitarian. A touching remembrance titled "A Great

Love Story Ends" came from radio personality and author Mary Margaret McBride, who, while writing a 1930 biography of Dwight Morrow, had gotten to know the Morrows quite well. Betty's passing, she said, "brought to a close my favorite real-life love-success story." McBride cited a fond description by daughter Elisabeth: "We were the most fortunate of children, for we knew we were dearly loved and wanted. But all their lives we realized that in the final analysis what really counted for those two was each other."

Elizabeth Cutter Morrow's funeral was held on Wednesday, January 26 at First Presbyterian Church, officiated by her minister, Rev. Dr. Bertram Atwood, and by the Morrows' long-time friend Dr. Henry Pitney Van Dusen, president of Union Theological Seminary. In attendance were notables such as Judge Learned Hand, Dwight Morrow's J. P. Morgan partners Thomas Lamont and Russell Leffingwell, and Smith College President Dr. Benjamin Wright. Numerous local politicians were there, as were board members from the many schools and charities with whom she had been associated. Mrs. Morrow's extensive household staff was present, as was her family, including son-in-law Charles Lindbergh, who had flown from Europe to attend.[18]

---

18 See both the seating chart for family and friends and the funeral program, located in the Appendix.

CHAPTER   8

THE LINDBERGHS

Up to now, this study has, of course, made several references to the Lindberghs. They are, after all, an extension of the extraordinary family that we've been studying—Anne, child of Dwight and Betty, native of Englewood, and Charles, the prominent in-law who spent much time there. They are a well-documented couple, and this chapter will make no pretense of trying to include all that the many existing biographies cover. However, there is still much the general public does not realize about the extent of their brilliant accomplishments. For many people, familiarity with the Lindberghs might be limited to Charles' epic 1927 flight to Paris, the 1932 kidnapping of the couple's firstborn, Charles Jr., and, to the extent that people are readers, Anne's bestselling 1955 book *Gift from the Sea*. It is our aim here to point out other salient features of their lives, beyond the headlines that most people are familiar with. As we do so, keep in mind that these very different people complemented each other as a powerful team. After considering them individually, we will conclude with a brief summary of the collaboration that made them another extraordinary American family created in Englewood.

I.

Many know only **Anne Morrow Lindbergh's** name without realizing her family story and connection to Dwight Morrow. More than once, when telling people that I've been writing a book about Dwight Morrow, I need to give Anne's full name and say "her father," before it registers whom I mean. Anne is a prominent figure on her own, whose many accomplishments have been documented in at least three books about her life, plus one about the couple:

David Kirk Vaughan's *Anne Morrow Lindbergh* (1988);

Dorothy Herrmann's *Anne Morrow Lindbergh: A Gift for Life* (1992);

Joyce Milton's *Loss of Eden: A Biography of Charles and Anne Morrow Lindbergh* (1996);

Susan Hertog's *Anne Morrow Lindbergh: Her Life* (1999). This book has been the subject of some controversy, as the author was never granted access to the Lindbergh papers housed at Yale University and was not approved to write a biography of Anne Lindbergh while she was alive.

Let us first consider Anne's literary achievements, before listing some of her accomplishments in aviation.

A. Literary Achievements

It was always important for Anne Lindbergh to have a dedicated place to write. Her husband, Charles, supported that wish and made sure that she had workspace either in their home or in a little cottage behind the house.

Charles and Anne Morrow Lindbergh at Lambert Field, St. Louis. Photograph by Ralph R. Rugh, Courtesy Missouri Historical Society Collections

Well before the best-known *Gift from the Sea*, Anne was, even more than her mother, a prolific writer. Five volumes of her diaries and letters were published during her lifetime; a final volume, edited by her daughter Reeve along with Reeve's brother Land, their niece Kristina Lindbergh, and their friend Carol Hyman, appeared 11 years after Anne's passing.

Bring Me a Unicorn: 1922-1928 (1971);

Hour of Gold, Hour of Lead: 1929-1932 (1973);

Locked Rooms and Open Doors: 1933-1935 (1974);

The Flower and the Nettle: 1936-1939 (1976);

War Within and Without: 1939-1944 (1980).

Against Wind and Tide: Letters & Journals, 1947-1986 (2012). These six books are a fascinating document of not only the Morrow and Lindbergh families, but also of cultural and political life in the first decades of the twentieth century.

North to the Orient (1935) documented the pioneering survey flight that she and Lindbergh made across Canada and Alaska to Japan and China. It went from late July to early October, 1931. The trip was successful as far as it went but was cut short by damage to the plane in the Yangtze River and the death of Anne's father, Dwight Morrow. The book won an inaugural National Book Award.

Listen! The Wind (1938) chronicled another ambitious survey flight that went from July 9 to December 19, 1933. It went eastward to Greenland and Europe, south to Africa, west to South America, and back north to the US, covering 30,000 miles. This book too won a National Book Award.

The Wave of the Future **(1940)** was the most controversial thing that Anne Lindbergh ever wrote. It addressed the same question of non-interventionism that her husband had championed as a spokesman for the America First movement. The book was followed by "Reaffirmation," a response to critics that appeared in the *Atlantic Monthly*. Both works were preceded by "Prayer for Peace," published in *Reader's Digest* in January, 1940. The piece was so popular that both isolationists and interventionists distributed reprints of it (MEM).

The Steep Ascent **(1944)** also chronicles a flight but without the description of exotic people and places. Rather, it is a fictional account of a trip the Lindberghs took to India as seen through the recollections of the novel's narrator. "In the thoughts and sensations of Eve Alcott, Lindbergh presents a complex study of a woman's sense of loss, fear, and renewal in the face of life-threatening conditions" (DKV 64).

Gift from the Sea **(1955)** was begun, Anne writes, "for myself, in order to think out my own particular pattern of living, my own individual balance of life, work and human relationships" (9). As before, she was trying to come to terms with her role and identity as wife, mother, and creative writer, all of which competed for her time and energy. Her task was "basically: how to remain whole in the midst of the distractions of life; how to remain balanced"

(29). Her meditations on this task were developed on the beach of the remote southwest Florida island of Captiva, and the images she used to focus her thoughts were the seashells whose names provide the titles for the book's chapters, e.g., Channeled Whelk; Double-Sunrise; Argonauta. Waiting for those treasures, Anne found, teaches patience and faith. While she wrote this book for herself, she found that it spoke eloquently to generations of readers who sought their own balance of life, work, and human relationships. The surprise best seller was later reissued in a 50th Anniversary Edition.

The Unicorn and Other Poems, 1935-1955 **(1956)** reprinted most of the poems that Anne had published in magazines such as the *Atlantic Monthly* and *Ladies Home Journal.*

Earth Shine **(1969)** is dedicated to the Lindberghs' efforts to reconcile the oft competing interests of technology and the environment. The little book is comprised of two essays that Anne wrote for *Life* magazine. The first featured wildlife observed on a 1966 trip to African game preserves; the second was based on the Lindberghs' VIP visit to Cape Kennedy, including a lunch with the astronauts, just before launch of the 1968 Apollo 8 mission to orbit the moon. In 2004 the Earth Shine Institute was formed in Fort Myers, Florida to create and support educational and cultural programs that further the balance between technological advancement and stewardship of the environment.

B. Aviation Achievements

- After their marriage in 1929, Anne Lindbergh rapidly entered her husband's world of aviation. He taught her to fly, while she studied navigation and earned a radio operator license. She was also a graceful presence that year in the start-up of Lindbergh's Transcontinental Air Transport (TAT).
- In 1930 she became the first woman to earn a US license as a glider pilot.
- Also in 1930, while seven months pregnant, she navigated for Lindbergh as he set a speed record for a flight from Los Angeles to New York.
- In 1931, on their trip to the Orient, she became the first woman to fly across the Pacific Ocean while helping with the survey tasks of the flight.
- In 1934 she received the Hubbard Medal from the National Geographic Society for serving as radio operator and copilot on the extensive 1931 and 1933 flights.
- She was co-pilot with her husband making pre-WW 2 trips to Germany, the Middle East, and Russia.

II.

Charles A. Lindbergh was arguably the world's most famous public figure, known first for his prodigious flying feats and years later for his support for the controversial America First efforts to keep the US from any involvement in World War II. As with Dwight Morrow, his astonishing accomplishments go far beyond what most people are aware of. We will list here a few of his other noteworthy achievements as complements to the larger Morrow story, but let us remember that they are exceedingly brief summaries of much longer stories. For many more details on the life of Charles Lindbergh, the reader is referred to extensive studies such as those by Scott Berg and Thomas Kessner.

A. Aviation Achievements

1. It is fair to say that no individual after the Wright brothers contributed more to the popularity and development of aviation than did Charles Lindbergh. Indeed, that was his stated goal returning from Paris: "I want to do all I can for American aviation. That is going to be my career" (TK 120). That goal was supported by copper magnate Daniel Guggenheim's Fund for the Promotion of Aeronautics that sponsored an astonishing **22,350-mile tour with the *Spirit of St. Louis*** to all 48 US states between July 20 and October 23, 1927. As reported by Scott Berg, Lindbergh "had stopped in eighty-two cities, spending the night in sixty-nine of them, where he had been honored at gala dinners. . . . He had flown 260 hours, delivered 147 speeches, and had ridden in 1,285 miles of parade. An estimated thirty million spectators had turned out to see him, one-quarter of the nation" (SB 169-170).

2. This flight was soon followed by the December **goodwill trip to Latin America.** As discussed in Chapter 5, the tour began in Mexico, where Lindbergh helped Dwight Morrow improve US-Mexican relations and, not incidentally, met his future wife. He continued to 15 other countries in South

and Central America and the Caribbean, concluding in early February, 1928.

3.   In 1928 Lindbergh pursued his dream of transcontinental air service beginning with a route from New York to California. He was the leading partner of a start-up called **Transcontinental Air Transport (TAT)** that cut in half the time required to span the country, from 96 to 48 hours. Because night flying was not advanced enough for passenger travel—few airports were equipped for night service, and light beacons needed for navigation along the way were rare—TAT flew only by day and put passengers on trains for the two overnight legs of the journey. As Robert Kirk points out, the railroads gave "TAT three very important public relation advantages: the railroads' reputation for safety, dependability, and punctuality. By connecting the new risky endeavor of flying with the traditional safety and dependability of the railroad, TAT established itself as safe, dependable, and fast" (RK 6).

For the two overnight rail segments, TAT used the Pennsylvania Railroad in the eastern part of the country and the Atchison, Topeka & Santa Fe Railway in the west. The westbound trip began with an overnight train from Pennsylvania Station via a special spur route to the Port Columbus (Ohio) airport terminal. Passengers were transferred to Henry Ford's multi-engine, corrugated metal airliner, the Ford Tri-Motor, nicknamed the "Tin Goose," for the daytime legs of the trip. The second overnight was from Waynoka, Oklahoma to Clovis, New Mexico with four more air legs to Los Angeles. The westbound trip began with a morning flight from Los Angeles and retraced the route back to New York, with train connections to Philadelphia, Baltimore, and Washington, DC. The first flights began in July, 1929.

Anne Lindbergh said of her involvement with TAT: "Really, this is much more fun than I imagined" (HGHL 50) and followed with a glowing recommendation of the operation:

"I am simply amazed at the detail that has gone into this TAT line. They give so much care to comfort and luxuries. All the conveniences and comforts are beautifully planned out. Such things as soup in the middle of the morning 'served aloft' and lunch, of course, and 'lemonade or tea' in the afternoon. And an aero-car to take you from plane to train for your night rides. And showers in the stations where you change. And a map given to each passenger so he may study the country" (HGHL 55).

TAT, the creation of which took over a year, was soon marketed as "The Lindbergh Line," and rightly so, for Charles lent far more than his name to the venture. He crisscrossed the continent many times, selecting the best locations for airfields and calculating the time needed for each leg of the journey. Lindbergh was handsomely compensated with a $10,000 annual salary and a $250,000 bonus at the start. Two years later, Lindbergh also teamed up with Juan Trippe, the founder of what would become Pan American Airways, where he served as a consultant for 40 years. After a merger with Western Air Express, TAT became T&WA and eventually evolved into TWA, Trans World Airlines.

4. The 1930s saw the Lindberghs make **numerous flights together**, beginning with the 1931 transpacific and 1933 transatlantic survey trips described in Anne's books. In 1935, seeking to escape the constant hounding by the press and continued threats to their family after the kidnapping, they moved first to England and then to France, returning only in 1939 on the eve of the outbreak of World War II. While abroad they continued to promote and research aviation as far away as India, Russia, and the Middle East. They also spent time in Greece, Italy, and most of all Germany, which they visited several times at the behest of the US military that sought to determine the capabilities of German aviation. No one was more able to assess those capabilities than Charles Lindbergh. He was recruited for this task by the American military attaché to Berlin, Major Truman Smith, who arranged access to numerous German airfields, factories, and aviators. Smith and his superiors were most grateful for the information gathered by Lindbergh, which served as a wake-up call for the underprepared US military. However, Charles' very positive public comments about the German people and their *Luftwaffe* (air force) were resented by many Americans who recognized the growing menace of Nazi Germany. The most controversial episode came on October 18, 1938 at the American Embassy in Berlin, where Lindbergh was surprised with an award presented by Air Marshall Hermann Goering by order of Adolf Hitler, the

prestigious Service Cross of the German Eagle. Lindbergh, who had received countless awards in many countries since his celebrated Paris flight, apparently thought little of it at that point, but as time went on, his critics interpreted the award and his failure to return it, as a sure sign of his Nazi sympathies.

This was his rationale for not returning the award: "It seems to me that the returning of decorations which were given in times of peace, and as a gesture of friendship, can have no constructive effect. If I were to return the German medal, it seems to me that it would be an unnecessary insult. Even if war develops between us, I can see no gain in indulging in a spitting contest before that war begins" (SB 381). The medal remains in the Lindbergh collection at the Missouri Historical Society in St. Louis.

5. Along with his continued quest to advance aviation, the 1930s saw Lindbergh become passionately involved in medical technology. This began when he asked physician friends why medical science could not repair the damaged heart of his sister-in-law Elisabeth Morrow. They introduced him to **Dr. Alexis Carrel** (1873-1944), a Frenchman who in 1912 had won the Nobel Prize for his technique of suturing blood vessels and was now a leading fellow at New York's Rockefeller Institute of Medical Research. Carrel explained that a mechanical pump was not feasible to circulate blood during surgery and that infection invariably crept into the system during experiments. What was needed, he said, was development of a perfusion pump to keep tissue and organs

alive outside of their organisms by circulating oxygenated blood or a sterile nutritious fluid across the tissue. Carrel had developed the fluid, but his primitive attempt at a pump was of no use.

When Lindbergh, a mechanical savant, immediately said he could do better, Carrel welcomed him into the Institute as a colleague. Whenever possible, Lindbergh drove from New Jersey to New York to work on the pump and assist Carrel with his other research. The two became fast friends and together published a book on *Culture of Organs*. In 1935, after four years of trial and error, Lindbergh completed the first successful perfusion pump, made of blown glass and with no moving parts. Their partnership was twice celebrated by *TIME* magazine, with a cover of Carrel in 1935 and one of Lindbergh and Carrel with the glass pump in 1938. For a short time that year, they were also neighbors off the of coast Brittany, at Saint-Gildas, where the Carrels lived, and Illiec, the tiny neighboring island purchased by the Lindberghs.

6. When the US was forced to enter World War II after Japan's attack at Pearl Harbor on December 7, 1941, the non-interventionist America First movement disbanded. It's chief spokesman, Charles Lindbergh, declared himself ready to serve in the military. However, because of his disagreements with and criticism of President Roosevelt, he was not allowed to serve on active duty and resigned his commission in the Army Air Corps. What then could be his **contribution to the war effort**? It was threefold:

- **Working for Henry Ford** at the gigantic Willow Run aircraft plant that produced the B-24 Liberator heavy bomber. Lindbergh moved his family to suburban Detroit while he advised on the development of the B-24, which initially had numerous quality control problems to overcome as managers and workers transitioned from automobile to aircraft production. He also volunteered for ten days of risky medical experiments at the Mayo Clinic to gauge human endurance at high altitude. That was followed by numerous test flights with the P-47 Thunderbolt fighter, which was greatly improved by Lindbergh's suggestions for high altitude flying.

- Consulting for the United Aircraft Corporation of Hartford and training pilots on the F4U Corsair, the Marines' top fighter plane in the Pacific. A company executive "recalled Lindbergh's taking his plane up and engaging in a high-altitude gunnery contest against two of the Marines' best pilots [and] the forty-one-year-old civilian 'outguessed, outflew, and out-shot' both his opponents, each practically half his age" (ASB 448).

- **Flying with the Navy** in the summer of 1944 in the South Pacific. While technically an "observer," "tech rep," and "adviser," Lindbergh completed 50 combat missions flying P-38s and Corsairs with the tacit approval of the military. Mostly he delivered bombs and strafed Japanese buildings and vessels in western

New Guinea, often dodging heavy anti-aircraft fire. Still, his greatest contribution was instructing pilots how to dramatically reduce fuel consumption, extending the combat radius by about 200 miles and the flying time by two hours or more. This enabled the US pilots to penetrate deeper into Japanese air space and more safely navigate the long flight home over water and hostile territory. It also attracted the attention of General Douglas MacArthur, who twice summoned Lindbergh to learn how the added range of American planes could help his planning for the campaign to retake Japanese held territory in the Southwest Pacific.

B. Literary Achievements

Charles Lindbergh became an **excellent writer**, tackling that task as he did many others, with focus and persistence. His first book, *We*, was a commercial success, but his second autobiographical description of the 1927 flight, *The Spirit of St. Louis*, on which he worked for years, was superb, winning the Pulitzer Prize in 1953. The aforementioned *Culture of Organs* was written together with Alexis Carrel and published in 1938. Only during and around the war years—from 1937 to 1945— did he keep a daybook, but those notes were extensive indeed, about 1,000 pages in print. In 1970 they were published as *The Wartime Journals of Charles A. Lindbergh.* Lindbergh's *Autobiography of Values* was published posthumously, in 1977.

III.

As we have pointed out, **Charles and Anne Morrow Lindbergh** were enormously talented and prolific individuals, but they formed a powerful team as well. Many of their pioneering aviation feats were done together, as documented in Anne's books, and both fliers were enshrined in the National Aviation Hall of Fame, he in 1967 and she in 1979. Their plaques can be viewed here:

Charles: https://nationalaviation.org/enshrinee/charles-augustus-lindbergh/

Anne: https://nationalaviation.org/enshrinee/anne-morrow-lindbergh/

They respected each other intellectually and regularly sought each other's comments as they wrote their books. In their last years together, the Lindberghs championed conservation efforts worldwide and sought to balance advances in technology with stewardship of the environment. In their honor, a foundation was formed to do that very thing. Its stated mission is defined thus:

In 1977, the 50th Anniversary year of Charles Lindbergh's epic New York-to-Paris flight, friends of the Lindberghs at The Explorers Club in New York City conceived the idea and General James H. Doolittle and Astronaut Neil Armstrong led a national campaign that resulted in the establishment of The Charles A. and Anne Morrow Lindbergh Foundation. Their intent was to honor the Lindberghs' pioneering contributions in aviation, exploration, conservation, sciences, and the humanities. Knowing the Lindberghs' vision of a balance between the technological advancements they helped pioneer, and the preservation of the human and natural environments they cherished, it was decided that this balance vision would become the cornerstone of the Foundation's programs. Ever since, the Foundation has strived to carry on the concept of balance, which was at the heart of the Lindberghs' philosophy for a lifetime, through the Lindbergh Grants Program, the Lindbergh Award, and other educational programs and publications.

Finally, their greatest collaboration was in raising their children, though with Charles' constant travel for his work, it was Anne who most kept things going at home.[19] Here are the Lindberghs' six children:

- Charles Augustus Jr. 1930-1932
- Jon Morrow 1932-2021
- Land Morrow 1937-
- Anne Spencer 1940-1993
- Scott Morrow 1942-
- Reeve Morrow 1945-.

---

19   After Anne's death in 2001, it was learned that Charles had fathered seven children with three women in Germany.

CONCLUSION

This book is subtitled "An Extraordinary American Family," and I trust that it is now evident why. What made them extraordinary began with the brilliant mind and sterling character of Dwight Morrow, but while the emphasis is on him, we must remember that his wife, Elizabeth, was a prominent public figure in her own right. Theirs was a great partnership and an enduring love story from which we can all learn. Their legacy also includes the four highly accomplished children—Elisabeth, Anne, Dwight Jr., and Constance—along with the Lindbergh and Morgan in-laws.

The secret of Dwight Morrow's great power, wrote his nephew, was that *he liked people.* That quality was, as we saw, evident in his attitude toward the Mexicans when he became Ambassador. It also led to his great success as a mediator, for people trusted him and were willing to follow his lead in negotiations. No man, Walter Lippmann told us, had the *complete trust* of so many different kinds of people.

Lippmann also called Morrow the *most talented* public man of his generation; he was likely the *most versatile* as well, reaching an elite level in four careers: law, high finance, diplomacy, and electoral politics. Beyond that, by dint of his great intelligence and relentless work ethic, he made himself an expert in the fields of prison policy, wartime logistics, naval treaties, and aviation.

Amherst classmate President Calvin Coolidge closed his tribute with a brief overview of Morrow's career that emphasized his *desire to serve*. "I have seen him develop into a ripe scholar, an able lawyer, a great businessman, a wise statesman, and a devoted husband, father and patriot. When most men would retire he seems always just beginning—beginning some new service for his friends and neighbors, for his Country and for humanity. It is the glory of the United States that it can produce such citizens" (HHH xiii).

The combination of brilliance and caring, talent and good will constitutes the *balance* that Dwight Morrow sought in his life. We saw that earlier in his love of Psalms 90 and 121 and in Philippians 4:8, read at his memorial service: "Finally, brethren, whatever is true, whatever is honorable, whatever is just, whatever is lovely, whatever is gracious, if there is any excellence, if there is anything worthy of praise, think about these things." To that we must add Plato's "Prayer of Socrates," another Morrow favorite read at the service, that wishes, "May the outward and inward man be at one." This balance of virtues was perhaps best expressed by Vice President Charles Dawes in his observation that "nature seldom decorates a man of *genius* with those *human qualities* and that *exceptional character* possessed by Dwight Morrow."

Elizabeth Cutter Morrow, a woman of great character, faith, and talent, was the ideal life partner for Dwight in their 28 years of marriage. She also distinguished herself in her almost 24 years as a widow, facing life's challenges with grace and, in Nicolson's word, "guts." The word *versatile* more than applies to Betty as well. She was wife, mother, grandmother; hostess, campaigner, public speaker; diarist, poet, patron of the arts; church and community leader, the "Englewood benefactor mourned by the world," as the 1955 headline proclaimed. Indeed, she achieved the lofty goal of her youth, to be "historical and social and domestic all at once."

My belief as a student at Dwight Morrow High School was that we all should know for whom the school was named, and why. I hope that this study will prompt alumni, current students, faculty, and, for that matter, all Englewood residents and interested readers everywhere to be inspired by the character, talents, and accomplishments of Dwight Morrow. At the same time, may we also recognize the enormous impact of Elizabeth Morrow and appreciate the local, national, and international history that was made by Englewood's most prominent residents in the first half of the twentieth century.

APPENDIX

I. Existing Literature on the Morrows

One of the purposes of this book is to commend to my readers for their future consideration works other than the three Dwight Morrow biographies cited in the Introduction. In addition, there is an abundance of good reading by and about his family. This section aims to illustrate the current state of research by amplifying numerous entries listed in the Bibliography.

A. More on Harold Nicolson, *Dwight Morrow*.

What then was so problematic about the "standard" Morrow biography? Harold Nicolson, a prolific writer, gives us a hint when he states in his published *Diaries and Letters 1930-1939* that "No book has caused me so much fuss and worry as this one." He calls his writing "heavy as lead" (197) and adds, "I am very disappointed in the book now that I read it *en masse*" (198). Even his verdict after a re-writing is muted: "I am not really discontented with the book."

Much insight into Nicolson's own character and the story of writing the biography is gained in Harold's letters and diary entries, as well as his son Nigel's extensive editorial comments. They reveal a strangely ambivalent relationship to his subject, strongly tinged by Nicolson's dislike of America and Americans, whom he calls "incurably suburban" (183) and "undiscriminating" (187), marked by "smarminess" and "eternal superficiality" (189). Especially irked by the sentimental cheerleading of the Morrows' Pittsburgh neighbors whom he meets during his research, Nicolson writes, "This sort of thing makes me loathe Morrow" (187). Later he admits to being possessed of "something really *unkind* . . . . I was conscious of a temptation to cause pain" (189). It is unfortunate that something Nicolson was *tempted* to say to the Morrow admirers, just to hurt them—namely, "Morrow was a shrewd and selfish little *arriviste* who had drunk himself to death" (189)—has been indiscriminately reported as his actual assessment of his subject, and it has caused Morrow's descendants no little discomfort. Morrow may have campaigned against Prohibition, but there is no evidence that Nicolson's comment was anything more than a meanspirited swipe at Morrow's adoring neighbors.

Still, several noted writers such as bestselling Bill Bryson and J. P. Morgan historian Ron Chernow have implied that Morrow's well-known absentmindedness was instead a manifestation of alcoholic stupor. Chernow twice cites Nicolson, but he credits another historian of Wall Street, John Brooks, for the above-cited "*arriviste*" remark from a letter to Nicolson's wife. Brooks for his part considers Nicolson's book "bland and syrupy" and says of the offending quote, "That would have been at least as much of a lie as the pap Nicolson actually wrote" (JB 111).

While Brooks saw the hypothetical quote in context, Bryson apparently did not, for he not only adopted the alcoholic narrative but also embellished it: "Morrow was not so much absent-minded as incapacitated by drink. He was, it appears, a hopeless souse" (145). These flippant words clearly fly in the face of the fierce work ethic and enormous accomplishments we have documented in the life of Dwight Morrow.

To be sure, Harold Nicolson does acknowledge those accomplishments, but even the superlatives are mixed with bizarre characterizations. Another letter from Englewood to Nicolson's wife in England illustrates that well: "Morrow is a Protean figure. There was about him a touch of madness, or epilepsy, or something inhuman and abnormal. Very difficult to convey, but certainly there. He had the mind of a super-criminal and the character of a saint. There is no doubt at all that he was a very great man" (186).

It is a fortunate by-product of his book that, because Nicolson was living with the family for months on end, we are granted an intimate glimpse of the family's life at a significant time for them and the country. The personal sympathy for Morrow that seems to be lacking in the Nicolson biography is present, however, in the accounts of Elizabeth Morrow and her celebrated daughter and son-in-law, Anne and Charles Lindbergh, in Nicolson's *Diaries and Letters*.

In 1934 the Morrows and Lindberghs were still dealing with a double loss: the premature death of Dwight Morrow in 1931 and the brutal kidnapping and murder of Charles A. Lindbergh, Jr. in 1932. Coincidently, two days before Nicolson arrived in America, Bruno Richard Hauptmann had been arrested for the crime. Thus, much of Nicolson's time with the family coincided with the ongoing police investigation of the kidnapping, the sensational trial, and the constant glare of publicity that began with Lindbergh's epic flight to Paris in 1927. To all that came another tragedy, the illness and early death in December, 1934 of Elisabeth Morrow Morgan, eldest child of Dwight and Betty Morrow. As Nicolson witnesses Mrs. Morrow cope with these triple traumas, his respect and concern for her is evident: "I feel quite bruised with pity for her. She seems so lonely in her misery, poor little thing. I do admire that woman. She never breaks down under these blows" (190).

With Mrs. Morrow sometimes absent, Nicolson is alone with the Lindberghs at the Morrow home, and his estimation of them is likewise very high: "I like the man. I dare say he has his faults, but I have not yet found them. She is a little angel" (183). He admires Lindbergh's devotion to his baby son, Jon, and adds, "It is all nonsense people saying that Lindbergh is disagreeable. He is as nice as can be. This morning he opened his heart to me on the subject of publicity. He absolutely loathes it" (184). Still, even as the couple deals with continued stress, "they are splendid in the way that they never intrude this great tragedy on our daily lives. It is real dignity and restraint" (184).

Nicolson's relationship to the Lindberghs bore fruit in two other ways. His favorable response to Anne's 1934 article published in *National Geographic* was a great encouragement to her budding career as an author. And when in late 1935 they fled the crush of publicity and the frequent threats to their young son, Jon, it was at Nicolson's English country home called Long Barn that they lived for two years with a sense of peace and security that had eluded them at home in America.

Later, however, when Lindbergh was embroiled in the America First isolationist controversy at the beginning of World War II, Nicolson's critical spirit again emerged in his writing about the aviator's public addresses. "Like so many others," Lindbergh responded, "(I expected something better from him), he attacks me personally rather than the things I advocate with which he disagrees" (WJ 279).

B. Dwight Morrow References in Other Studies.

1.   Dwight Morrow is prominently mentioned in several works devoted to other notables, such as Amity Shlaes' biography *Coolidge* (2013). Shlaes highlights the relationship between Morrow and the future president that began at Amherst College (Class of 1895) and lasted until Dwight's untimely death in 1931. The two friends were standouts in a group of talented, ambitious young people and similar in their earnest manner: "Coolidge's fellows suddenly saw in him something like what they saw in Dwight Morrow—that rare ability to turn potential humiliation into good cheer" (48). She points out how absorbed Morrow became in politics as his classmate rose through the ranks, and in 1920 he enthusiastically supported Coolidge as he sought the Republican nomination for President. "Coolidge's small team fought to the end.

Morrow converted his hotel room into a lobbying office. He was so enthusiastic that he followed the delegates around; there was even a photo of Morrow pursuing a delegate wearing only a small towel around his waist" (200).

Warren Harding won that nomination and election, but Coolidge was chosen as Vice President, and at Harding's death in 1923, Coolidge ascended to the presidency. "Coolidge clearly valued Amherst but handed out few spots to Amherst men" (284), a fact the Morrows found curious, yet they did not exploit their closeness to the president for personal gain. Eventually, however, Coolidge would tap Morrow for two positions that did much to shape what publisher Henry Luce would later dub the American Century.

In 1925 he appointed him a member of a board—of which Morrow would be elected chairman—to decide what role aircraft had in the US defense. And in 1927 he named him Ambassador to Mexico at a time when relations between the two countries were frayed and potentially violent. One of Morrow's first moves at the embassy was to invite the world-famous aviator Charles Lindbergh to Mexico on a goodwill trip, from which developed his relationship to the ambassador's daughter, Anne, the flier's future wife. Those two appointments did much to influence American aviation. And, as Shlaes poignantly points out in reference to the Lindbergh kidnapping, "The Coolidges felt a kinship with their friends' daughter and son-in-law. For all the challenges that celebrity imposed on an ex-president, the challenges for a Lindbergh were even greater. In his autobiography Coolidge had made the argument that his son had lost his life[20] because his father had been president. It was certain that the Lindbergh baby had lost his life because of his father's fame" (450).

2. Three chapters in Ron Chernow's landmark study *The House of Morgan* (1990), #12 "Odyssey," #13 "Jazz," and especially #15 "Saint," feature Dwight Morrow in his role as partner at J. P. Morgan. After mention of Morrow's humble upbringings and superior career at Amherst, classmate of future President Coolidge, Chernow writes, "Morrow performed spectacularly at 23 Wall and mastered every subject through sheer diligence" (289). He also highlights Morrow's continuing relationship to Calvin Coolidge, his sponsorship of aviation and Charles Lindbergh, his great success as ambassador to Mexico, and the inevitable conflict between the worlds of high finance, politics, and diplomacy.

3. Those interested in a scholarly analysis of Dwight Morrow's work in Mexico will want to consult these four works:
    •   Howard F. Cline, *The United States and Mexico.*
    •   L. Ethan Ellis, "Dwight Morrow and the Church-State Controversy in Mexico."
    •   Stanley Ross, "Dwight W. Morrow, Ambassador to Mexico"; and "Dwight Morrow and the Mexican Revolution."

---

20 Coolidge's younger son, Calvin Jr., had died as the result of a mishap at the White House.

- Richard Melzer, "The Ambassador *Simpatico*: Dwight Morrow in Mexico 1927-30."

These three works bring additional information:

- Gouverneur Morris, "On Morrow in Mexico." This is a blog from a Coolidge website. It reviews the feature film *For Greater Glory: The True Story of Cristiada*, which touches briefly on the role of Coolidge and Morrow in the Cristeros conflict.
- Susan Danly, ***Casa Mañana: The Morrow Collection of Mexican Popular Arts***.
- Sir Arthur Salter, ***Recovery***, which is dedicated to Dwight Morrow.

4. The gold standard for Lindbergh studies, A. Scott Berg's ***Lindbergh*** (1998), understandably has many references to the aviator's father-in-law. Berg explains how Dwight Morrow became acquainted first with Lindbergh's mother, Evangeline, when a guest of the Coolidges, and then with the flier himself upon his triumphant return from Europe. Morrow brokered payments for Lindbergh and his financial backers as well as raising $50,000 for the tour that Lindbergh made with "The Spirit of St. Louis" to promote aviation in all 48 states. He also became his adviser at J. P. Morgan. This sound relationship led to Lindbergh's goodwill visit to Mexico.

In addition to many biographical notes on Morrow's career, Berg nicely relates the Morrows' move to their grand new home in Englewood, Anne's engagement and marriage there, the birth of Charles A. Lindbergh, Jr., the launching of Morrow's campaign for the United States Senate, and the overwhelming outpouring of respect and sympathy at the Senator's early death at age 58. "Mrs. Morrow," writes Berg, "would emerge as a national figure, one of the prime exemplars of twentieth-century women who devoted their lives to public service through volunteerism."

Other Lindbergh studies, such as Thomas Kessner's *The Flight of the Century: Charles Lindbergh and the Rise of American Aviation* (2010), mention the aviator's prominent father-in-law, especially as an advocate for aviation and an advisor to Lindbergh.

5.   Three studies of Anne Morrow Lindbergh—an analysis of her major works, plus two biographies—also have extensive references to Dwight Morrow, including many of the biographical milestones featured in other works.

David Kirk Vaughan's monograph in Twayne's United States Authors Series, *Anne Morrow Lindbergh* (1988), after listing many of Morrow's stellar achievements, focuses on his qualities as "an energetic and indefatigable worker," a "moderate by nature," and a "mediator." Vaughan links these qualities to Anne, stating that her father "was the first and most lasting influence on her career as a writer" (2-3). One prime example of that is Anne's controversial treatise on the isolationist views of her husband, *The Wave of the Future* (1940), which "owed its genesis to the philosophical views of her father, Dwight Morrow, primarily his middle-of-the road, practical approach to solving international disputes" (52).

Dorothy Herrmann in *Anne Morrow Lindbergh: A Gift for Life* (1992), calls Morrow "a brilliant and charming man who was not only a mesmerizing conversationalist but also a superb diplomat who lived and breathed his profession." She also cites Anne's parents' relationship—"a devoted, perfectly matched couple, so passionately in love with each other that their all-absorbing happiness often had made their children feel excluded from their lives" (84).

Susan Hertog in *Anne Morrow Lindbergh: Her Life* (1999) highlights the symbiosis of the Morrow-Lindbergh alliance: "Anne's marriage to Charles made Dwight the perfect candidate for just about everything. . . . With his son-in-law at his side, Morrow could woo voters from a platform beyond party affiliation: 'Peace through progress.'"

6. *A Distant Moment: The Youth, Education, & Courtship of Elizabeth Cutter Morrow* (1977), a charming chronicle and loving tribute to her mother written by the Morrows' youngest daughter, Constance Morrow Morgan, affords us insight into the early life and career of Dwight Morrow. If ever there were an intimate glimpse of an age long gone, it is the description of their courtship begun at the neighboring colleges of Amherst and Smith and lasting a full ten years before marriage in 1903. Morrow's being "married to the office" was alternately a source of humor and concern to his colleagues and loved ones. It was, writes Constance, "deep, complex, and sometimes sinister" (183), and a key to understanding his enormous achievements and, perhaps, his untimely demise.

7. The six published collections of diaries and letters by Anne Morrow Lindbergh understandably have numerous references to her father, although they are scattered.

    Anne's mother, Elizabeth Cutter Morrow, was also a prolific diarist, whose works we have cited extensively, especially in chapter 7. Of course, she had much to say about Dwight. However, from the decades she recorded in her diaries, only three and a half years were ever published, in a private, extremely small print run called *The Mexican Years: Leaves from the Diary of Elizabeth Cutter Morrow* (1953).

    The Wartime Journals of Charles A. Lindbergh (1970) have a few references to Dwight Morrow and many to Betty and other family members.

8. In addition to the two special tributes to Dwight Morrow cited earlier, by Walter Lippmann and the US Congress, two others following his death in 1931 stand out in their assessment of Morrow's brilliance, character, and salutary influence on a culture wary of and weary from corrupt politicians.

    *   Morrow's nephew Richard B. Scandrett, Jr., in his *Memorial of Dwight Whitney Morrow*, cited the international press's "universal tribute such as few men of any generation have received." Despite his enormous prestige, writes Scandrett, Morrow "was a simple man, and those who knew him best regarded him as a man without personal ambitions. . . . The secret of [his] great power cannot be better summarized than in the three words: *He liked people*. He liked people not only

in the objective, but in the personal sense. He liked individuals."

- Also in 1932, the **Amherst Graduates' Quarterly** published an appreciation by three of Morrow's classmates, focusing on his career preparation at the college, his work as an Amherst trustee, and his sterling character, the epitome of "an Amherst gentleman."

9. Beyond the routine references to Morrow in the various New York and New Jersey dailies, three other periodicals made prominent mention of him: *TIME* magazine; *The New Yorker*; and the New York publication **Outlook and Independent** (19281832), a merger of the news magazines **Outlook** and **Independent**.

Dwight Morrow's own published book, *The Society of Free States* (1919), a collection of columns that originally appeared in the New York *Evening Post*, was written in the aftermath of World War I and focused on peace plans such as the League of Nations. Its overarching question is, "Can the conflict between world order and national independence be reconciled?"

Morrow also authored a lengthy, scholarly introduction to a book by his Amherst mentor Anson Morse, *Parties and Party Leaders* (1923) and an article in *Foreign Affairs* on **"Who Buys Foreign Bonds?"** (1927).

Some few newsreel images of Morrow exist online, as well as his minor and unfortunate cinematic depiction in *For Greater Glory: The True Story of Cristiada* (2012), cited above.

II. Stories of Morrow's Abstraction, aka Absentmindedness

"A favorite relates how on a particularly busy day he rang for Arthur Springer, his secretary, who responded and stood by the desk waiting. Morrow suddenly looked up, and said, 'Will you please ask Mr. Springer to come in?' The secretary circled around the desk and stood again, waiting. Finally Morrow looked up at him. 'Oh, Springer,' he said, 'will you please write all that down for me?'" (MMM 155).

"'We were dressing for dinner in the same room at the University Club,' [the much taller Thomas] Cochran relates, 'and Dwight got interested in something he was telling me. In his absorption, he began to put on my clothes instead of his own. He had on the shirt before I noticed him and then I let him go ahead just to see how long it would be before he'd realize what he was doing. The sleeves of the shirt hung over his hands but he never seemed to know it. He put on the trousers, vest, and finally the coat. At that point, he looked down in a puzzled way, for his hands had completely vanished. When I burst out laughing, he laughed, too, enjoying the joke as much as I did'" (MMM 156).

"Seward Prosser was once toastmaster at a dinner at which Morrow spoke. In his introduction Mr. Prosser told the most famous of the 'abstraction' stories. He said that Mr. Morrow got on a train and when the conductor, who knew him, said: 'That'll be all right, Mr. Morrow.' But Morrow went on hunting. The conductor said again, 'Don't bother, Mr. Morrow;' and Mr. Morrow answered 'I must find that ticket. You see it's got the name of my destination on it and I've got to find out where I'm going'" (MMM 156-157).

"At a dinner party given, in later years, in the house of Thomas Lamont, an incident occurred which is illustrative of Morrow's habits of abstraction. At the outset of this dinner, Dwight Morrow helped himself to a large green olive. He held this olive, as conversation developed, between his thumb and forefinger; soup turned into fish and fish in its turn gave place to entrée; still did Dwight Morrow wave that olive in the air. From time to time he would pass it from his right to his left hand. The other guests, as Morrow continued his rapt monologue, became fascinated by that olive with which he punctuated his remarks; he made sweeping gestures with that olive indicative of the extent of British collateral or of the vast era of the American investing public; he made precise dabs with that olive when distinguishing between different methods of discounting; he pawed the air with that olive when assuring Lord Reading that the situation was not as yet beyond control. Coffee had arrived and the men rose to pass into the smoking room. Morrow was still explaining, holding his olive (by now a dried object with one bite in it) triumphantly aloft. It was then that Metcalfe, the Lamont butler, felt that it was time to intervene. He advanced toward Morrow with a plate extended. 'Your olive, Mr. Morrow'—it was only then that Morrow, still unconscious, put it down" (HN 174).

III. Dwight Morrow's Last Will and Testament

LAST WILL AND TESTAMENT

OF

DWIGHT W. MORROW

Died October 5, 1931

Admitted to Probate by the Surrogate of the County of Bergen, State of
New Jersey, on the 23rd day of October, 1931, on which date
Letters Testamentary were issued to Elizabeth C. Morrow
and Bankers Trust Company

The Evening Post Job Printing Office, Inc., 154 Fulton St., New York, N. Y.

Dwight Morrow's Last Will and Testament Courtesy Amherst College Archives and
Special Collections

I, Dwight W. Morrow, of Englewood, New Jersey, declare this to be my Will, revoking all other wills and codicils heretofore made by me.

First: My Executors shall first pay my debts, funeral expenses and expenses of administration.

Second: I then bequeath:

A. To my sisters, Agnes M. Scandrett, Alice Morrow, and Hilda M. McIlvaine, and to my brother, Jay J. Morrow, Fifty Thousand Dollars ($50,000), to each of them;

B. To my wife's sisters, Annie S. Cutter and Edith Cutter Yates, Twenty-five Thousand Dollars ($25,000), to each of them; to my wife's mother, Mrs. Annie E. Cutter, Twenty-five Thousand Dollars ($25,000), but if she predeceases me then this bequest shall not lapse, but shall go to her said two daughters, Annie and Edith, equally, or to the survivor of such two;

C. To my friend, George D. Olds, now President of Amherst College, Twenty-five Thousand Dollars ($25,000), but if he predeceases me this bequest shall not lapse, but shall go to his wife, Marian Olds; to my friend and Amherst College classmate, Charles T. Burnett, now a Professor at Bowdoin College, Twenty-five Thousand Dollars ($25,000); to my friend, Frederick J. E. Woodbridge, now a Professor at Columbia University, Twenty-five Thousand Dollars ($25,000); and to my friend and associate, Martin Egan, of the City of New York, Twenty-five Thousand Dollars ($25,000);

D. To my secretary, Arthur S. Springer, Twenty-five Thousand Dollars ($25,000);

Courtesy Amherst College Archives and Special Collections

Appendix

2

E.   To the TRUSTEES OF AMHERST COLLEGE, a body cor-
     porate established by law in the Commonwealth of
     Massachusetts, TWO HUNDRED THOUSAND DOLLARS
     ($200,000). Without limiting such Trustees' dis-
     cretion in their use of this absolute bequest, I here
     mention my preference that this bequest be added
     to the general endowment of the College, the income
     to be applied to the maintenance and, if possible,
     to the increase of professors' salaries at such
     College;

F.   To the TRUSTEES OF THE SMITH COLLEGE, a corpora-
     tion established by law in the Commonwealth of
     Massachusetts, TWO HUNDRED THOUSAND DOLLARS
     ($200,000), to be part of the endowment funds of
     such College;

G.   To the SMITHSONIAN INSTITUTION, City of Wash-
     ington, District of Columbia, ONE HUNDRED THOU-
     SAND DOLLARS ($100,000), to be part of its en-
     dowment funds;

H.   To the TRUSTEES OF COLUMBIA UNIVERSITY IN THE
     CITY OF NEW YORK, FIFTY THOUSAND DOLLARS
     ($50,000), to constitute a fund, the income of
     which is to be applied, from time to time, to the
     uses and purposes of its SCHOOL OF LAW;

I.   To THE UNION THEOLOGICAL SEMINARY IN THE
     CITY OF NEW YORK, FIFTY THOUSAND DOLLARS
     ($50,000), to be part of its endowment funds;

J.   To the ASSOCIATION FOR IMPROVING THE CONDI-
     TION OF THE POOR, New York City, New York,
     FIFTY THOUSAND DOLLARS ($50,000), to be part
     of the endowment funds of such Association, the
     net income to be expended, from time to time, for
     the general charitable and benevolent purposes of
     the Association;

3

K. To the ENGLEWOOD HOSPITAL ASSOCIATION, Englewood, New Jersey, FIFTY THOUSAND DOLLARS ($50,000), to take and hold the same in trust, as part of the endowment funds of such Association, the net income of this bequest to be expended, from time to time, for the general charitable and benevolent purposes of the Association;

L. To the SOCIAL SERVICE FEDERATION OF ENGLEWOOD, Englewood, New Jersey (formerly the "Civic Association of Englewood, New Jersey"), TWENTY THOUSAND DOLLARS ($20,000), to take and hold the same in trust, as part of the endowment funds of the Federation, the net income of this bequest to be expended, from time to time, for the general charitable and benevolent purposes of the Federation;

M. To the CITY OF ENGLEWOOD FREE LIBRARY, Englewood, New Jersey, TEN THOUSAND DOLLARS ($10,000), to take and hold the same in trust for the benefit of such Library, the net income of this bequest to be expended, from time to time, in the purchase of books, prints, pictures, maps and manuscripts, preferably those dealing with local history, all in furtherance of the educational purposes of the Library.

THIRD: All the residue of my estate, including any lapsed legacies, and subject to the payment of all transfer, succession or inheritance taxes, either against my estate or the bequests made in this Will, I devise and bequeath to my wife, ELIZABETH C. MORROW, her heirs and assigns, to be her absolute property.

I make no provision in this Will for my children and make my wife my residuary legatee, with every confidence in her that she will provide for herself and my children

4

when and as she may determine is in her and their several best interests. This expression of my confidence in her neither qualifies this residuary bequest nor impresses a trust character thereon, the bequest being absolute and free of all restrictions.

FOURTH: I appoint my wife, ELIZABETH C. MORROW, and BANKERS TRUST COMPANY, of the City of New York, my Executors. If my wife does not survive me, I appoint my brother, JAY J. MORROW, Executor in her place. No bond or other security shall be required of her, him or it as such Executrix or Executors.

FIFTH: I authorize and empower my Executors:

a. To sell, at public or private sale, and to mortgage, lease and convey, all or any part of my estate, both real and personal, at such times and upon and for such terms and conditions as they may deem best;

b. At the risk of my estate and without responsibility to them, in their discretion, to continue, and to turn over in payment of any bequest or devise in this Will, any stocks, bonds or other securities in which at the time of my death any portion of my estate may be invested;

c. In their discretion, to settle, compromise and adjust any and all claims in favor of or against my estate;

d. In their discretion, to vote, deal and consent, in person or by proxy, as to all stocks or other securities of my estate;

e. In their discretion, to continue to completion any investment or undertaking of mine pending, but not completed, at the time of my death, and, in that connection, to borrow and pledge securities of the estate to secure any such borrowings.

5

SIXTH: I direct my Executors to accept, without question, any statement which may be rendered them by the firm of J. P. MORGAN & COMPANY, of which I am a member, both as to any interest I may then have in such firm (or in any predecessor firm bearing that name), and as to the amounts, if any, due from or to me as to such firm or any such predecessor. Such statement shall be conclusive upon my Executors and upon all other interested persons.

SEVENTH: Should my wife not survive me, then I appoint as the guardian of the property and persons of my minor children surviving me, my brother, JAY J. MORROW. No bond shall be required of him as such guardian.

IN WITNESS WHEREOF, I subscribe my signature, under seal, declaring this to be my last Will and Testament, this twenty-fourth day of January, nineteen hundred and twenty-seven.

DWIGHT W. MORROW (L.S.)

The foregoing, on the date thereof, was signed, sealed and declared by DWIGHT W. MORROW, to be his last Will and Testament, in the presence of the undersigned, who then, as witnesses thereof, at his request and in his presence, and in the presence of each other, subscribed our signatures.

CHARLES J. FAY
        Residing at 53 East 66th St., N. Y. City.
WALTER S. ORR
        Residing at 136 East 36th St., N. Y. City.
PAUL G. PENNOYER
        Residing at Duck Pond Road, Glen Cove,
        L. I., N. Y.

4961—B

Courtesy Amherst College Archives and Special Collections

Appendix

IV. Lewis Haskell's Recollections of the Morrows and Lindberghs at North Haven

My first recollections of the Dwight Morrow family was when they spent part of one Summer at the Etta Noyes" (Freeman Smith, now David Cooper). This was probably 1924 or '25. Later, I recall Mother being quite excited when she learned the Morrows had been looking at the old Grant farm with the idea of buying, which they did in

Soon there was all kinds of activity. Whenever we visited my Aunt, Uncle and Cousins, there was either exciting news or something to show us`: all the surveyor stakes; the string drawn tight between the batter boards; the digging commenced, then the cement forms put in; then the studding up and the roof rafters on. Soon there was an immense new house standing where a short time before there had been an old cellar hole and a few raspberry bushes. The house was located on the old Deacon Sam Brown farm and was referred to as Deacon Brown's Point. All this was only the beginning.

The workmen soon began re-modeling the old Grant homestead, completely re-doing the South East end, and I was amazed at the beautiful large kitchen my Aunt now had. The old barn came down. This was one of the bigger barns on the Island, and, in its place, they built a new building. On the North end was a roomy workshop; in the middle a modern tie up for several cows; and, on the South end, a garage. On the second story, all the space was for storing hay.

To the East of the farm house was a large four bay garage with apartment rooms on the South end and a good sized apartment on the second floor. Then they built a guest house several hundred feet West of the new cottage. All of these buildings were of a simple architecture; shingled and painted white with green shutters. The chimneys were also painted white with a black top stripe.

Aside from all the hustle and bustle of the carpenters, masons, plumbers and electricians, there was the landscape garden crew, from Bar Harbor Nurseries; planting trees and laying out the grounds and gardens. In no time at all, the old farm was transformed into a beautiful estate with a small golf course, swimming pool and tennis court. Because we visited with my Aunt, Uncle and Cousins nearly every weekend, I had an opportunity to watch all this transpire and was as excited about the transformation as, I'm sure, they were.

Some of the workmen I remember were: The contractor, Owen Lermond; his son, John; the Fish brothers, who were the masons; Parker Stone, the boss plumber; Avery Dyer, Alfred Dyer, Chester Dyer, Clarence "Chick" Stone, Raymond "Skilley" Stone, Irven Stone, Carl Bunker and Russ Crabtree were the carpenters I remember. Others, I recall were: William Billadue, Frank Gowell, Corydon Brown, Lawrence Grant, Owen Grant and Fred Howard. Peterson's crew, from Vinalhaven, did the wiring.

When the Morrows arrived for the Summer, they brought their household help with them from Englewood, New Jersey. The chauffeur and his wife, Alfred and Josephine Burke, I got to know the best; they had the apartment over the garage. I believe the butler may have had the downstairs apartment.

I, like the rest of North Haven, was extremely pleased and excited when the news that one of the Morrow daughters, Ann, was engaged to the national hero of that time, Charles A. Lindbergh, and, like everyone else, I looked forward to getting a glimpse of him. I recall the excitement of knowing they were honeymooning on the yacht, Mouette, in the general area of Penobscot Bay. Then there came the day I saw Lindbergh working around an airplane he had probably rented and landed on the golf course right in front of the big Morrow Cottage. He was as tall and skinny as his picture showed him. After this, that piece of ground was referred to as the Lindbergh landing field. It was a short field and, I'm sure, required a good pilot to get in and out of there which he did on many occasions.

Courtesy of the North Haven Historical Society, North Haven, Maine

2.

In 1931, we moved to an old farm just a short distance from the Morrow estate and it was common for me to visit my Cousins. From these visits, I met up with the Lindbergh nurse maid, Betty Gow, as she cared for little Charles, a beautiful blond baby. I was terribly shocked when the news of his kidnapping came. The aftermath of all that was reflected at North Haven with the necessity of body guards and the nuisance of reporters when the Lindberghs were on the Island.

The yacht, Mouette, gave the Morrow family much pleasure. Her first Captain was Floyd Duncan; later Carl Bonney Quinn; and still later, Murray Stone.

A boat house was built on the shore of the Grant Cove, big enough to house the Mouette and a 21' Knock-a-bout sail boat.

My good friend, Hugh Parsons, became Mrs. Morrow's personal caddy after Ronald Gillis gave up the job. Hugh enjoyed the job and his association with Mrs. Morrow and all the help. It was from this job he left to enlist in the Army in the Summer of 1940.

It was a sad time for me when my Uncle died in *1946* and my Aunt and Cousins left the old home where I had spent many happy times with them.

The new caretaker was Owen Brant who had worked there for the Morrows from the beginning. Mrs. Morrow died in *1955* , and, soon after the property was sub- divided and much of it sold, buildings demolished or moved, and, in some instances re-modeled so that it is impossible to imagine today the once beautiful estate.

1. Guest room
2. Large living room
3. Constance's bedroom
4. Mr. & Mrs. Morrow's bedroom
5. Guest room
6. Dining room
7. Kitchen

Courtesy of the North Haven Historical Society, North Haven, Maine

V. Seating Chart for Mrs. Morrow's Funeral

CENTER AISLE

PEW							
1	AML	DWM	CWM	ANNIE	DAVE & AUNT E.	ROB	KAY SULLIVAN SHELDON
2	STEPHEN	SARAH	FAITH RHID.	SCOTT	CONNIE	ANNE	LAND REEVE E.
3	AUBREY	CAL	MARGOT	KATHARINE LEIGHTON	EDWIN McILVAINE	RUTH VOORHEES	REBEKAH GREATHOUSE / MASTER LEIGHTON
4	FRED VOORHEES	KENRIC LEIGHTON	RICHARD SCANDRETT	MARY SCANDRETT	DWIGHT SCANDRETT	JEANNIE SCANDRETT	SANDY SCANDRETT
5	DR. ROSEN	HAZEL ROSEN	CONNIE CHILTON	BETTY VAN DUSEN	DOROTHY APPLEGATE	ROSA HUNT	
6	PRES. WRIGHT	MRS. WRIGHT	ANNETTA CLARK	DOROTHY ALMY	LILLIAN COURAND		

TRANSEPT AISLE

Courtesy Susan M. Kenney

VI. Printed Program for Mrs. Morrow's Funeral

𝔉𝔦𝔯𝔰𝔱 𝔓𝔯𝔢𝔰𝔟𝔶𝔱𝔢𝔯𝔦𝔞𝔫 𝔠𝔥𝔲𝔯𝔠𝔥
ENGLEWOOD, NEW JERSEY

BERTRAM deHEUS ATWOOD, Minister
ROBERT I. MILLER, Associate Minister
JOHN WRIGHT HARVEY, Organist and Choirmaster

S E R V I C E

January 26, 1955

for

E L I Z A B E T H   C U T T E R   M O R R O W

May 29, 1873   January 23, 1955

Courtesy Susan M. Kenney

Appendix

```
ORGAN   PRELUDE

CHORAL  INTROIT

          If through unruffled seas,
            Toward heav'n we calmly sail,
          With grateful hearts, O God, to Thee
          We'll own the fav'ring gale.

          But should the surges rise,
            And rest delay to come,
          Blest be the sorrow, kind the storm,
          Which drives us nearer home.


OPENING SENTENCES

THE COLLECT

THE LORD'S PRAYER          (All uniting)

SCRIPTURE READINGS                        Micah VI:6,8
                                      Philippians IV:8

HYMN - 'Dear Lord and Father of mankind'        No. 302
                                      Stanzas 1, 4, 5

          (The people standing)


PSALM XC

PSALM CXXI        (The people seated and uniting)

          I will lift up mine eyes unto the hills;
            From whence cometh my help?
          My help cometh from the Lord
            Which made heaven and earth.
          He will not suffer thy foot to be moved;
            He that keepeth thee will not slumber.
          Behold, he that keepeth Israel
            Shall neither slumber nor sleep.
          The Lord is thy keeper;
            The Lord is thy shade upon thy right hand.
          The sun shall not smite thee by day,
            Nor the moon by night.
          The Lord shall preserve thee from all evil;
            He shall preserve thy soul.
          The Lord shall preserve thy going out and thy
                                              coming in
            From this time forth, and even for evermore.


ROMANS VIII: 28-39
```

Courtesy Susan M. Kenney

A PRAYER OF ST. AUGUSTINE: *(Read by the Minister)*

O Thou Good Omnipotent, Who so careth for every one of us, as if Thou caredst for him alone; and so for all, as if all were but one! Blessed is the man who loveth Thee, and his friend in Thee, and his enemy for Thee. For he only loses none dear to him, to whom all are dear in Him who cannot be lost. And who is that but our God, the God that made heaven and earth, and filleth them, even by filling them, creating them. And Thy law is truth, and truth is Thyself. I behold how some things pass away that others may replace them, but Thou dost never depart, O God, my Father supremely good, Beauty of all things beautiful. To Thee will I entrust whatsoever I have received from Thee, so shall I lose nothing. Thou madest me for Thyself, and my heart is restless until it repose in Thee.

HYMN - *'I know not what the future hath of marvel or surprise'* Stanzas 2 and 3, No. 282

(Sung by the Choir)

A READING FROM *'PILGRIM'S PROGRESS'*

HYMN - *'For all the saints who from their labors rest'* (First tune) No. 429

(The people standing)

THE PRAYER OF THANKSGIVING *(The people seated)*

THE PRAYER OF COMMITMENT *(The Minister)*

O Lord, support us all the day long, until the shadows lengthen and the evening comes, and the busy world is hushed, and the fever of life is over, and our work is done. Then in Thy mercy grant us a safe lodging, and a holy rest, and peace at the last; through Jesus Christ our Lord. Amen.

THE BENEDICTION

RECESSIONAL HYMNS *(The people standing)*

* * * * * * *

Leading the Service are the Rev. Henry Pitney Van Dusen, President of Union Theological Seminary, and the Rev. Bertram deHeus Atwood, Minister of First Presbyterian Church.

The ushers are some of those who served on the official boards of the Church during the period when Mrs. Morrow was an Elder.

Courtesy Susan M. Kenney

ACKNOWLEDGMENTS

I am indebted to several people connected with the Morrow family and their legacy, none more so than Margaret Eiluned Morgan, whose mother, Constance Morrow Morgan, was the youngest of Dwight and Elizabeth Morrow's four children. Ever since we first met at an Earth Shine Institute event several years ago, Eiluned has been a great help and encouragement to my work, furnishing numerous suggestions, first for my Morrow-Lindbergh article and now for the manuscript of this book. She has been most generous with helpful information, sharing glimpses into her family's history and connecting me with people and resources that would assist my research.

Eiluned's cousin, Reeve Lindbergh, was also kind enough to review this manuscript, and I thank her for sharing her expertise as Lindbergh family representative.

Susan McIlvaine Kenney, in several extended conversations, shared fascinating stories of her Morrow-McIlvaine heritage and several images of family documents displayed in the book.

Frances Levine, former President and CEO of the Missouri Historical Society, encouraged me to submit for publication in the MHS *Gateway* magazine my research on Dwight Morrow's service as United States Ambassador to Mexico. I also thank her for reading and offering positive suggestions for this current book.

The Elisabeth Morrow School has twice welcomed my wife and me for a visit, and current Head of School Marek Beck has greatly encouraged the publication of this book.

Love and thanks go to my wife, Roberta, for accompanying and assisting me on various research trips, for her excellent insights on the various stages of writing, and for supporting my belief that the Morrows' story is most worthy of telling.

For research assistance and for sharing and granting permission to use documents, photos, and other illustrations, special thanks go to:

Karen Kukil and Kate Long of Smith College's Special Collections Department;

Peter Nelson and Mike Kelly of Amherst College's Special Collections Department;

Lori Thompson of Marshall University's Special Collections Department;

Christopher Gordon and Lauren Sallwasser of the Missouri Historical Society;

Leslie Taylor and the Englewood Public Library;

Irmari Nacht and the Englewood Historical Society;

Jacqueline Curtis and the North Haven Historical Society;

Queenie Viglione and the Captiva Island Historical Society;

Shelly Wimpfheimer of the Englewood Community Chest;

Brian Regrut, Jack Dannemiller, and Lee Southard for many helpful publishing suggestions;

Frank Gutbrod for the excellent design and layout of the book.

BIBLIOGRAPHY

BOOKS

Berg, A. Scott. *Lindbergh*. New York: G. P. Putnam's Sons, 1998.

Bouton-Goldberg, Bobbie, et al. *Englewood and Englewood Cliffs*. Charleston, SC: Arcadia Publishing, 1998.

Brooks, Jonathan. *Once in Golconda. A True Drama of Wall Street 1920-1938*. New York: Wiley, 1999.

Bryson, Bill. *One Summer: America, 1927*. New York: Doubleday, 2013.

Chernow, Ron. *The House of Morgan: An American Banking Dynasty and the Rise of Modern Finance*. New York: Grove Press, 1990.

Cline, Howard F. *The United States and Mexico*. Cambridge: Harvard University Press, 1953.

Danly, Susan. *Casa Manaña: The Morrow Collection of Mexican Popular Arts*. Albuquerque: University of New Mexico Press, 2002.

Falzini, Mark W. and James Davidson. *New Jersey's Lindbergh Kidnapping and Trial*. Charleston, SC: Arcadia Publishing, 2012.

Hermann, Dorothy. *Anne Morrow Lindbergh: A Gift for Life*. New York: Ticknor & Fields, 1992.

Hertog, Susan. *Anne Morrow Lindbergh: Her Life*. New York: Doubleday, 1999.

Howland, Hewitt H. *Dwight Whitney Morrow: A Sketch in Admiration*. New York, London: The Century Co., 1930.

Kessner, Thomas. *The Flight of the Century: Charles Lindbergh and the Rise of American Aviation*. New York: Oxford University Press, 2010.

Kirk, Robert F. *Flying the Lindbergh Line: Then and Now*. Bloomington, IN: AuthorHouse, 2013.

Lindbergh, Anne Morrow. N.B. Her six volumes of diaries, letters, and journals are given here neither in alphabetical order nor by date of publication but in the chronological order of the years they cover.

---. *Bring Me a Unicorn: Diaries and Letters of Anne Morrow Lindbergh 1922-28*. New York: Harcourt Brace Jovanovich, Inc., 1972.

---. *Hour of Gold, Hour of Lead. Diaries and Letters of Anne Morrow Lindbergh: 1929-1932*. New York and London: Harcourt Brace Jovanovich, 1973.

---. *Locked Rooms and Open Doors. Diaries and Letters of Anne Morrow Lindbergh: 1933-1935*. New York and London: Harcourt Brace Jovanovich, 1974.

---. *The Flower and the Nettle: Diaries and Letters of Anne Morrow Lindbergh, 1936-1939*. New York and London: Harcourt Brace Jovanovich, 1976.

---. *War Within and Without. Diaries and Letters 1939-1944*. New York and London: Harcourt Brace Jovanovich, 1980.

---. *Against Wind and Tide: Letters and Journals 1947-1986*. New York: Pantheon Books, 2012.

---. *Dearly Beloved*, New York: Harcourt, Brace & World, Inc., 1962.

---. *Earth Shine*. New York: Harcourt, Brace & World, Inc., 1966.

---. *Gift from the Sea*. New York: Pantheon Books, 1955.

---. *Listen! The Wind*, New York: Harcourt, Brace & World, Inc., 1938.

---. *North to the Orient*. New York: Harcourt, Brace & Co., 1967.

---. *The Steep Ascent*, New York: Harcourt, Brace & Co, 1944.

---. *The Wave of the Future,* New York: Harcourt, Brace & Co, 1940. Lindbergh, Charles A. *The Spirit of St. Louis*. New York: Charles Scribner's Sons, 1953.

---. *The Wartime Diaries of Charles A. Lindbergh*. New York: Harcourt Brace Jovanovich, Inc., 1970.

Lindbergh, Reeve. *Under a Wing: A Memoir*. New York: Simon & Schuster, 1998.

Lippmann, Walter. *Public Persons*. Ed. by Gilbert A. Harrison. New York: Liveright, 1976.

---. *Public Philosopher: Selected Letters of Walter Lippmann*, ed. John Morton Blum. McBride, Mary Margaret. *The Story of Dwight Whitney Morrow*. New York: Farrar & Rinehart, 1930.

McClure, Marc Eric. *Earnest Endeavors: The Life and Public Work of George Rublee*. Westport, CT: Praeger, 2003.

Milton, Joyce. *Loss of Eden: A Biography of Charles and Anne Morrow Lindbergh*. New York: HarperCollins Publishers, 1993.

Morgan, Constance Morrow. *A Distant Moment: The Youth, Education, & Courtship of Elizabeth Cutter Morrow*. Northampton, MA: Smith College, 1978.

Morrow, Dwight W. *The Society of Free States*. New York and London: Harper & Brothers Publishers, 1919.

---. "Introduction." In Morse, Anson Daniel. *Parties and Party Leaders*. Boston: Marshall Jones Co., 1923, vii-xlii.

---. "Who Buys Foreign Bonds?" *Foreign Affairs*, January, 1927. Morrow, Elizabeth Cutter. *Diaries*. Smith College Special Collections.

---. *The Painted Pig: A Mexican Picture Book*. New York: Alfred A. Knopf, 1930.

---. *Quatrains for My Daughter*. New York: Alfred A. Knopf, 1931.

---, with William Spratling. *Casa Mañana*. Croton Falls, NY: The Spiral Press, 1932.

---. *The Mexican Years: Leaves from the Diary of Elizabeth Cutter Morrow*. Croton Falls, NY: Spiral Press, 1953.

Nicolson, Harold. *Dwight Morrow*. New York: Harcourt, Brace and Company, 1935.

---. *Diaries and Letters: 1930-1939*. Ed. by Nigel Nicolson. New York: Atheneum, 1966.

Seventy-second Congress First Session. *Memorial Services Held in the House of Representatives of the United States, Together with Remarks Presented in Eulogy of Dwight W. Morrow,*

Late a Senator from New Jersey. Washington: United States Government Printing Office, 1932.

Shlaes, Amity. *Coolidge*, 2013. New York: HarperCollins Publishers, 2013.

Sloan, Alfred P. *My Years With General Motors*. New York: McFadden Books, 1965.

Vaughan, David Kirk. *Anne Morrow Lindbergh*. Boston: Twayne Publishers, 1988.

White, E. B. *One Man's Meat*. Gardiner, ME: Tilbury House, Publishers, 1997.

ARTICLES

"The Air Investigation: Army & Navy." *TIME*, 6 (15), October 12, 1925, 10-

"Ambassador Extraordinary." *The New Yorker*. October 15, 1927, 18-19.

Amherst Graduates' Quarterly. 1932.

A. F. C. [*sic*] "Backstage in Washington." *Outlook and Independent*, July 16, 1930, 418; July 30, 1930, 496; February 25, 1931, 291.

Davis, Norman. "Dwight Whitney Morrow." Englewood Historical Society, 2011.

"Effects of a Groundswell." *TIME*, Vol. 16 (Issue 13), September 29, 1930.

Ellis, L. Ethan. "Dwight Morrow and the Church-State Controversy in Mexico." *The Hispanic American Historical Review*, Vol. 38, No. 4 (Nov., 1958), 482-505.

Gouverneurmorris. "On Morrow in Mexico." On Morrow in Mexico | The Importance of the Obvious (crackerpilgrim.com), September 22, 2014.

Housum, Robert. "Robert Housum's History of the Novel Club 1896-1926." www.TheNovelClub.org.

Hye, Allen E. "Morrow, Mexico, and MHS: The Lindbergh Link." *Gateway*. Vol. 41, No.1, Spring 2021, 26-35.

Melzer, Richard. "The Ambassador *Simpático*: Dwight Morrow in Mexico 1927-30." In Ronning, C. Neale & Albert P. Vannuci, *Ambassadors in Foreign Policy: The Influence of Individuals on U.S.-Latin American Policy*. New York, Westport, CT, London: Praeger Publishers, 1987, 1-27.

Mitchell, Jonathan. "The Little Giant: Some Notes on Dwight W. Morrow." *Outlook and Independent*, July 2, 1930, 323-325, 355-357."

Morrow, Dwight W. "The First Milestone." In *An Amherst Book: A Collection of Stories, Poems,*

Songs, Sketches and Historical Articles of Alumni and Undergraduates of Amherst College. Ed. by Herbert Elihu Riley. University of California Libraries, 1896.

Ross, Stanley R. "Dwight W. Morrow, Ambassador to Mexico." *The Americas* Vol. 14, No. 3 (Jan. 1958), 273-289.

---. "Dwight Morrow and the Mexican Revolution." *The Hispanic American Historical Review*, Vol. 38, No. 4 (Nov., 1958), 506-528.

Scandrett, Richard B., Jr. "Memorial of Dwight Whitney Morrow." January 1, 1932.

Schuker, Stephen. "Dwight Morrow" in *American National Biography* (Cary, NC: Oxford University Press, 1998), vol. 15, 928.

OTHER MATERIALS

For Greater Glory: The True Story of Cristiada, 2012 film.

Vintage Newsreel Clips of Dwight Morrow:

1. This link takes you to five historic videos: https://digital. tcl.sc.edu/digital/collection/MVTN/search/searchterm/ Morrow%2C%20Dwight%20W.%20(Dwight%20 Whitney)%2C%201873-1931./field/subjec/mode/exact/ conn/and

   - Charles Lindbergh in Mexico
   - Ambassador Morrow Visits Ranch
   - Morrow Country Home
   - U.S. Delegation to Naval Conference (2 videos, both with sound)

2. These two clips report on the death and funeral of Dwight Morrow. https://www.pond5.com/stock-footage/ item/75313247-death-senator-dwight-morrow-new-jersey-1931 https://www.pond5.com/stock-footage/item/ 75769004-wealthy-businessman-and-ambassador-dwight-morrow-given-final.

3. This clip shows Elisabeth Morrow teaching Mexican children when her father was US Ambassador in Mexico City. https://www.youtube.com/watch?v=mhdqdMlyAhY